A Year of FLOWER WREATHS

MALIN BJÖRKHOLM

A Year of FLOWER WREATHS

SIMPLE FLORAL ARRANGEMENTS FOR ALL SEASONS

BATSFORD

For Jakob

Contents

Foreword

FLOWERS AND WREATHS follow us throughout life. Wreaths are used as a symbol for both happiness and sorrow; perhaps that's why they are so popular.

My life changed one day in April 2020 to never again be the same. The memories from this day are fragmented pictures without sound or other sensory impressions. I remember lying on the ground shouting, yet all I remember is silence. I remember the emergency services arriving, but I don't have any memory of sirens. It's all a vacuum.

This was the day when we found our child dead in his room. Our son, who soon should have turned 18, suddenly ceased to exist. Our considerate boy, who had grown into an affectionate young man. He, who always put the needs of others before his own. His heart suddenly stopped beating, without any forewarning whatsoever.

The time that follows I only have faint memories of. Months of grief passed and the summer came and went. Little sister learned to cycle and big brother turned 20, we swam and visited the cousins. I didn't recognise myself. All my creativity and inspiration had vanished. The little energy that was left, was used to take care of my family.

I strongly felt I didn't want to feel like this for the rest of my life. I was worried that grief would consume me and take over my whole being. Thanks to my inner strength, and through counselling, I slowly started to find a way to handle my grief and find room for it.

Eventually my desire to create returned. Much to my delight, since my creativity is such a big part of my personality. My passion for the home and garden – and creating beautiful environments – became my therapy. Working with my hands gave me new energy and a break from my thoughts. On my Instagram profile, I got a lot of appreciation for what I did. To inspire others is something that I have always found very rewarding and it is a major driving force for me.

This book is a tribute to my son. My love for him is just like a wreath; infinite, and it's not something that death can take away from me. I know that he would have been proud of where I am today, and that realisation gives me strength. Grief is always by my side, but life has good moments and I can take joy in them.

I hope that when you read this book you will be inspired to start creating your own wreaths and that my tips will give you the courage and strength to try.

Love, Malin

Longing for spring

AS SOON AS CHRISTMAS is packed away and January has begun, I start longing for spring. I want to go out and dig in the garden, get dirt under my nails, fill pots with lovely pansies and turn my face towards the spring sun.

The winters where I live on Öland, Sweden are often grey and brown. We rarely get snow – at least not for any extended periods of time – so when the Öland wind whistles around the corners of the house, I long for the light to return.

I satiate my longing by filling the house with budding grape hyacinths and crunchy tulips. Then I make a wreath from evergreen plants, reed, birch and hazel branches, together with dried flowers.

I like to buy spring bulbs in January. I place them indoors in little pots and decorate with a few branches. Spring flowers are probably the ones I long for the most during the year. They give me hope that nature will come to life again.

If the winters are mild, I start digging as early as January. That bed that was never planted the previous year can suddenly become reality in the winter darkness. I love planning for spring's upcoming garden projects and I always think: this year is the year thar I will manage to do lots of things. I compile lists and sketch out plans for things to be built and planted.

As soon as the sun is out on a cold February day, I take my cup of tea and enjoy it sitting by the wall of the house. In my beloved greenhouse, not much sun is needed to make it lovely and warm, so it's often possible to sit there early in the season. I start by filling the greenhouse with spring bulbs, pansies and primulas – they do fine since it never gets as cold as outdoors.

Spring on Öland always offers a wonderful floral abundance, gorgeous blue and white meadows of blue and wood anemones. When the spring sun shines, I pack a picnic basket and take a walk out to my favourite places together with my family.

Twig pot wreath

In early spring, when nature hasn't yet burst into delicate greens and the spring bulbs haven't popped out of the ground yet, I plant pots with pansies and flowering narcissus outside the door. I like to decorate the pots with extra twigs, for example, a wreath made from bilberry stems. The wreath will also give extra support to the narcissus' leaves that otherwise easily fall outwards.

LEVEL: EASY

MATERIALS
Florist wire
Wire cutters
Floral tape
Myrtle wire, green
Secateurs
Plant pot

FLOWERS/FOLIAGE
**Bilberry stems or
 other fine twigs**
Spring bulbs

1 Take two lengths of florist wire and join them together using floral tape. Pull the tape lightly so that it gets tacky and sticks to the wire.

2 When you're halfway through, add more wire to make the frame longer and continue wrapping with tape.

3 Add more lengths of florist wire and wrap them together until the wire is long enough to fit as a wreath around your plant pot.

4 Bend the wire into a ring and twist the ends together. Secure with a bit of floral tape.

5 Attach the myrtle wire by wrapping it around the ring and twisting the end.

6 Start constructing the wreath by adding a bunch of bilberry stems to the ring and securing in place with myrtle wire.

7 Continue adding more bilberry stems. Cover the ends of the previous stems with the next batch of material to keep them hidden.

8 When you reach the end, lift up the first bunch of bilberry and tuck the stems under.

9 Turn the wreath over and cut the wire with the wire cutters.

10 Secure by 'sewing' a couple of stitches into the wrapped wire – thread the wire through a few times to secure it in place.

11 Place the wreath on top of a pot filled with spring bulbs.

Dense wreath in lovely pastel tones

It can be hard to find good materials for wreaths in the spring. When that happens, I go out to my garden and cut a few sprigs of box that I complement with a few bought flowers – for example, pink rice flower and apricot-coloured wavyleaf sea lavender. Light pastels will brighten up this season. The delicate, green colour of the box will also give a lovely spring feel. Even though I love large, bushy wreaths, they have their time and place. A compact wreath will give a neater impression and can often be simpler to make as well. This cute wreath will fit perfectly on my black cupboard in the greenhouse.

LEVEL: MEDIUM

1 A metal ring has a fairly slippery surface, so I always wrap it in floral tape. This will make the surface a bit tacky so the material won't slip. To do this, tear off a bit of floral tape and secure one end to the ring. Wrap the tape around the ring, lightly pulling the tape as you wrap to activate the glue and make sure the tape sticks.

2 Attach myrtle wire to the ring. Wrap the wire around and twist the end to secure it in place.

3 Start by adding little sprigs of box to the ring, then wrap a couple of times with myrtle wire so that it is secured in place.

4 Continue adding flowers and leaves along the ring, always making sure to cover the stems of the previous layer.

5 When you reach end of the wreath, lift the first layer of box and tuck the stems under.

6 Turn the wreath over and cut the wire with wire cutters. Secure by 'sewing' a couple of stitches into the wrapped wire.

7 Hang the wreath using string.

Keep in mind!
Common box tends to have an unpleasant smell, so I recommend that you don't bring the wreath indoors. Alternatively, use large-leaf box instead, since this variety is unscented.

MATERIALS
Metal ring
Floral tape
Myrtle wire, green
Wire cutters
String for hanging

FLOWERS/FOLIAGE
Box
Rice flower, pink
Wavyleaf sea lavender, apricot

Bushy spring wreath

I have a soft spot for big, bushy wreaths – wreaths that are allowed to take up space and that aren't so structured – where branches and flowers are very welcome to stick out in a playful way.

Here, I have started with a base of birch branches and complemented with more branches for a lovely spring feel. I have chosen to mix a lot of different materials to make it a very personal wreath.

There are a lot of nice materials that are green all year round and work well in wreaths, such as ivy and box. Mimosa both smells lovely and dries beautifully, and broad-leaved statice and wavyleaf sea lavender retain their colour perfectly, even after they've dried. To finish, I have complemented with some flax, dried poppy seed pods and hare's tail.

MATERIALS
Metal ring
Reel wire, black
Wire cutters

FLOWERS/FOLIAGE
Birch branches
Box
Broad-leaved statice
Flax
Hare's tails
Ivy
Mimosa
Small poppy seed pods
Wavyleaf sea lavender

LEVEL: MEDIUM

1 Start by covering a metal ring with flexible birch branches. This is partly to get a thicker base and partly to let the branches stick out so they are visible in the wreath.

2 Attach black reel wire to the metal ring.

3 Add birch branches around the base and wrap in place fairly loosely.

4 Place a few sprigs of box on top of the birch branches and wrap with the wire a couple of times.

5 Continue placing material, making sure that the stems from the previous step are covered.

6 Repeat around the whole wreath, varying greens and flowers. Make sure some branches are sticking out to provide variety.

7 To make the wreath bushier, try using materials of mixed length.

8 When you reach the end, lift the first layer of box and tuck the stems underneath to secure.

9 Turn the wreath over and cut the wire with wire cutters. Secure by 'sewing' a couple of stitches into the wrapped wire.

Spring flowers and moss wreath

Is there anything lovelier than the warmth returning in the spring? When I'm warmed by spring's first sunrays, I can feel my energy being restored.

I love planting spring bulbs in pots in the garden. Even if they haven't had a chance to come up in the beds yet, it's lovely to be able to enjoy these cute little flowers. Many varieties stand the cold well, although they don't want to go too many degrees below freezing.

Outside my kitchen window I have a garden table that I decorate according to the season. Here, I place a wreath made of moss and twigs, which acts as a nest for spring bulbs, such as grape hyacinths and narcissus.

LEVEL: EASY

1 Cover a straw wreath base with moss and secure it lightly in place with myrtle wire. Don't bind it too hard, or the wire will become visible.

2 Cut thicker branches into smaller pieces using secateurs. I like to use branches from older fruit trees, such as apple or pear trees. They are so wonderfully knotty and often have lichen growing on them.

3 Place the branches on top of the wreath, letting them stick out over the edges (both the outside and the middle). Secure the branches in place with lengths of coarse u-shaped florist wire.

4 Add ivy to the wreath, securing it in place with coarse u-shaped florist wire.

5 Place the wreath on a table.

6 Place spring bulbs in the middle of the wreath, either with or without pots. The bulbs will keep without soil, so you can take them out of the pots and remove some of the soil if you prefer.

7 Start by placing the tallest flowers in the middle and the shorter grape hyacinths in a ring around them.

8 Fill in any gaps with moss.

MATERIALS
Straw wreath base
Myrtle wire, green
Secateurs
Florist wire
Wire cutters

FLOWERS/FOLIAGE
Branches covered with
  lichen, preferably
  thicker ones
Grape hyacinth
Ivy
Moss
Narcissus

Spring flowers in eggshells

Isn't it lovely when spring finally arrives and all the spring flowers brighten up beautifully? A walk in the spring sun gives me so much energy and inspiration to make something.

Little spring flowers are wonderful, but they can also be difficult to place in a vase with their short stems. Here, I have created a wreath made of eggshells to put delicate spring flowers in.

LEVEL: EASY

1 Empty the eggs, breaking off as little of the shell as possible.

2 Wash off the red stamp on the eggshells using distilled vinegar.

3 Glue the eggshells together into a ring using a glue gun.

4 Add some water to the eggshells.

5 Place little spring flowers such as scilla and wood anemones into the eggshells.

MATERIALS
Eggshells
Distilled vinegar
Glue gun

FLOWERS/FOLIAGE
Scilla
Wood anemones

Mimosa wreath

Sun-yellow mimosa reminds me of the Mediterranean Sea, and stirs up my longing for sun and warmth. In the spring, I often use this wonderful flower in bouquets and wreaths. This mimosa wreath can be hung inside and dries beautifully; a few small sprigs of mimosa also spread a lovely scent. Mimosa can be kept over winter as a pot plant too.

LEVEL: MEDIUM

1 Start by wrapping a metal ring with floral tape. Secure the tape and lightly pull it so that it gets tacky and sticks to the ring. Wrap around the whole ring to prevent the flowers from sliding around.

2 Attach myrtle wire to the ring by wrapping it around and twisting the ends together.

3 Divide the mimosa into smaller pieces.

4 Place a couple of mimosa sprigs on the ring and secure by wrapping the myrtle wire a couple of times around the stems.

5 Place the next bunch of flowers so that the stems of previous bunches are hidden, and secure in place with myrtle wire.

6 Repeat until the whole ring is covered, overlapping and covering the previous bunches as you go.

7 When you reach the end, tuck the stems of the final bunch under the first bunch of mimosa to hide them.

8 Turn the wreath over and cut the wire with wire cutters. Secure by 'sewing' a couple of stitches into the wrapped wire.

MATERIALS
Metal ring
Floral tape
Myrtle wire, green
Secateurs
Wire cutters

FLOWERS/FOLIAGE
Mimosa

FACT FILE TOOLS AND MATERIALS

WREATH BASES

Wreath bases come in all kinds of materials and sizes. I usually choose a base according to the placement and look of the finished wreath. When choosing a base, bear in mind that all wreaths become bigger when they're finished, since the material will add a lot of bulk.

Bases made of straw are the most common and are the easiest for starting out when making wreaths. They come in many different sizes. I recommend 28–32 cm (11–12½ in) for a door wreath.

Metal rings are my favourite base and I often use these for thinner wreaths. For door wreaths, a 25–30 cm (9⅞–11¾ in) ring is good. For larger wall-hanging wreaths, I use 40 cm (15¾ in).

There are ready-made bases made from willow or wreaths covered in artificial moss available to buy. You can also make a base yourself using flexible branches, such as birch or willow twigs.

For extra large wreaths, I often use hula hoops. They are good value for money and very solid, so they can take the weight.

When I need to make a wreath to an exact size, I make a ring out of steel or aluminium wire.

WIRE

The most common wire is reel wire, which you can get hold of in both DIY stores and garden centres. The wire comes either with a plastic green coating or untreated. The green wire doesn't rust on the outside like the untreated one can do. Reel wire is a coarse wire that is best suited for straw bases and the use of coarser plant materials.

For metal rings and softer plant materials, I use green myrtle wire. It is thinner and a lot more flexible than reel wire and is therefore better suited to more delicate materials.

Silver myrtle wire is a decorative wire that I use when the thread will be seen. It's not as durable as green myrtle wire and can therefore be pulled apart. Myrtle wire is best sourced from a good floristry shop or garden centre.

When the wire will be visible, I also sometimes use florist wire that is coated in paper or string.

TAPE

Floral tape is a tape made from paper that I use partly to join lengths of florist wire for wreath bases, but also to prevent the plant material from sliding on metal rings. The tape isn't tacky on the roll, so you have to pull it lightly to make it stick.

TOOLS

When making wreaths, a good pair of secateurs is the best tool. I have different secateurs that are suitable for softer and heavier materials respectively.

For flowers, I use a pair of floral scissors (flower snips), or a sharp knife.

For florist wires, I recommend wire cutters, since wire will damage secateurs.

WREATH MATERIALS

In spring, it can be a little bit grey out in nature and it can seem difficult to find nice material for wreaths. But there are so many pretty things available if you look properly.

Branches often make the base for my wreaths during this season. Birch branches are flexible and perfect for making wreath bases (see page 24). Willow and pussy willow are also good for bases and to use in wreaths generally.

At the beginning of the year, I usually include evergreen needles in spring wreaths. I mix conifers with dried flowers and evergreen leaves together with branches of hazel: a mix between winter and spring.

Different kinds of moss also work well as a base for spring's wreaths and these can be decorated with branches and common houseleek, for example.

The further into spring it gets, the stronger my craving for lighter wreaths and wonderful spring colours becomes. Evergreen leaves of box, ivy and a few bought olive branches can become a good base.

I complement this with pastel-coloured broad-leaved statice and wavyleaf sea lavender. Around this time, it's still possible to buy eucalyptus, which I like to use in wreaths. I love its grey-green colour and the shape of the leaves.

Flowering spring bulbs are also lovely. The bulbs can last without soil, as they have all the nutrition they need in the bulb. I like to use small narcissus together with grape hyacinth or tulips.

Decorations, such as feathers and eggshells, make wonderful spring wreaths (see page 34).

Reeds still stand nicely by the sea during spring and go well with last season's dried flowers.

In Öland's pine forests there are plenty of blueberry bushes whose stems are green and beautiful even without leaves, so I often seek these out for spring wreaths.

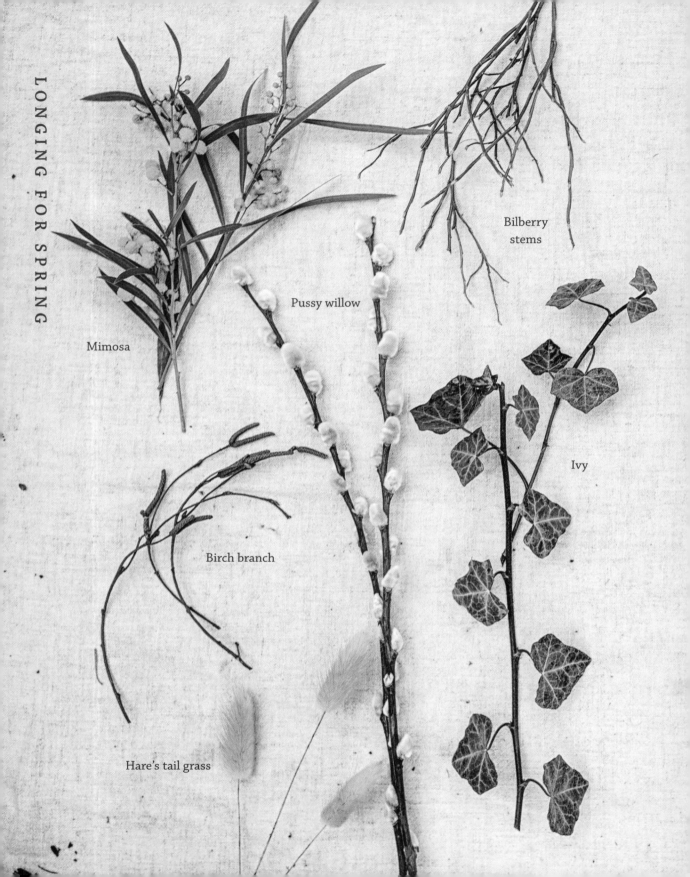

Mimosa

Pussy willow

Bilberry
stems

Ivy

Birch branch

Hare's tail grass

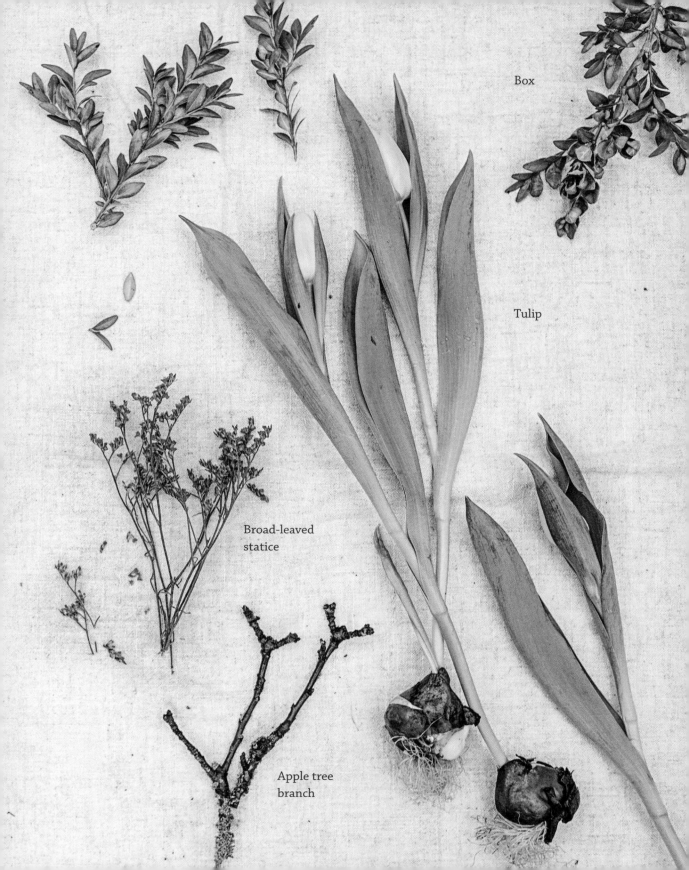

Box

Tulip

Broad-leaved
statice

Apple tree
branch

Budding greenery

EVERY YEAR IT IS fascinating to watch nature fully explode in greenery. As soon as the warmth returns, all the leaves come out and the flowers reach for the light. Not long ago it was grey and pretty boring, but everything can change in a matter of just a few days. The growth power of nature is completely magical.

Lovely cherry blossom, like pink clouds, and fragrant apple blossom, so transient, but wonderful. I make the most of it and enjoy every second, putting branches into vases and letting the wonder of nature move in.

Under my apple tree, the tulips are flowering among the ivy. The effort of planting the bulbs in the autumn has paid off. I pull out weeds, add fertiliser and watch with excitement as the beds come to life.

Pots with pansies and beautiful leaves, such as maidenhair and clover, are placed out on the garden table. Shortly they will be joined by beautiful summer flowers, such as gaura and chocolate cosmos.

The geraniums have been moved into the greenhouse after their winter rest, which is once again filling with a lovely scent. The sun warms up my greenhouse nicely and I like to take a break here from my daily chores.

The planters are prepared for sowing, the soil is improved with new nutrients. Soon, beautiful flowers and vegetables will grow here. The plants are moved out slowly to harden up and are dug into the ground as soon as the night frost is gone.

We eat a picnic by the sea and have our first dip of the year. The children finish school and we listen to beautiful summer songs.

Soon, midsummer time is here and I make crowns of beautiful flowers. I fill little vases with cute flowers from the garden and the roadside, for the summer's beautiful table settings.

The whole summer is ahead of us with the promise of a time of enjoyment.

Summer ceiling crown

Is there anything lovelier than a dinner in the greenhouse underneath a crown of greenery and flowers? I love bringing summer indoors for table settings, and hanging flowers from the ceiling is a wonderful way to do this. This green wreath keeps well, and you can change out the flowers when they have wilted.

LEVEL: ADVANCED

1 Start by wrapping a metal ring with floral tape. Secure the tape and pull it lightly so that it gets tacky and sticks to the ring. Wrap around the whole ring to prevent the flowers from sliding around.

2 Cut two equal lengths of string, for hanging the ceiling crown.

3 Tie the string to the ring in four places, then tie them over each other in the middle of the ring so that they form a cross.

4 Attach test tubes by wrapping them in place with wire-reinforced string. Wrap a cross over the tube and the ring so that they are securely fastened.

5 Attach a vine of ivy to the ring using florist wire.

6 Wrap vines around the wreath to cover the metal ring.

7 Attach branches of butcher's broom with florist wire to fill in any gaps where needed. Let the ends stick out to create some visual variety.

8 Place clematis and Michaelmas daisies in the test tubes filled with water.

9 Hang the ceiling crown over the table.

MATERIALS
Metal ring
Floral tape
Scissors
String
Test tubes
**String reinforced
   with wire**
Florist wire

FLOWERS/FOLIAGE
Butcher's broom
Clematis
Ivy
Michaelmas daisies

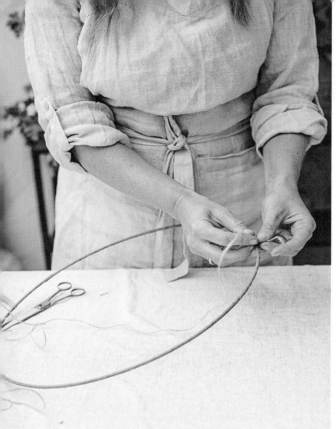

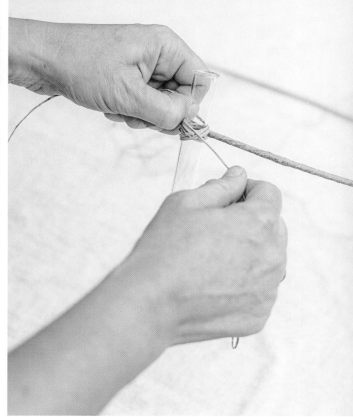

Tip!

The green leaves will last for a long time. You can change out the flowers when they have wilted, or alternatively leave the wreath beautifully green.

Test tube wreath

Making a wreath with summer flowers can be difficult when the sun is shining, as the flowers tend to wilt. But having sweet little flowers in a wreath on the wall works perfectly if you use test tubes that you can fill with water to help the flowers flourish. You can also easily swap the flowers out when they have wilted.

LEVEL: EASY

1 Cut a good length of string and tie it to the metal ring.

2 Wrap the string around the ring, criss-crossing it and securing tightly.

3 Thread test tubes into the string, placing every other tube over, and every other under, each row of strings.

4 Add a little water to the tubes and place flowers in them, for example clematis, billy button and lisianthus.

5 Attach a length of string in a loop to the top of the ring and hang the wreath up on a wall or in a window.

MATERIALS
String
Scissors
Metal ring
Test tubes

FLOWERS/FOLIAGE
Billy button
Clematis
Lisianthus

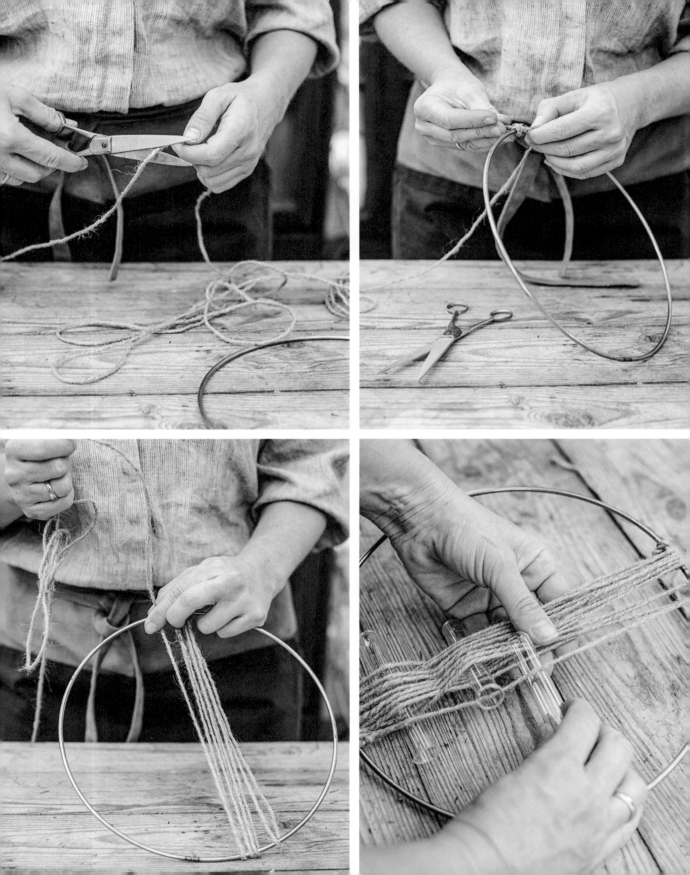

Midsummer flower crown

On midsummer morning, I wake up early, sit down in the dewy grass and make wreaths for me and my daughter; little summer bouquets that together form a flower crown. For me, it doesn't feel like midsummer without wreaths.

LEVEL: MEDIUM

1 Measure the head's circumference; the wreath base should be approximately 4 cm (1½ in) smaller for the crown to sit comfortably.

2 Join two lengths of florist wire together with floral tape. Pull the tape so that it gets tacky and wrap it around the wire.

3 When you get halfway, add another length of florist wire to make the base as long as your measurement from step 1.

4 If required, add more wire to make the wreath longer. Measure to check that it is long enough.

5 Make a loop at each end of the florist wire, then twist the end.

6 Attach the myrtle wire right underneath one of the loops.

7 Place pistacia and a softer flower over the loop to hide it, then secure by wrapping myrtle wire around the stem.

8 Continue placing material over the stems of previous flowers along the whole length of the wire.

9 At the other end, turn some of the flowers the other way and place them over the loop to hide it.

10 Cut the myrtle wire and secure it around the florist wire.

11 Insert a silk ribbon into both loops.

12 Tie the flower crown comfortably at the back of the head.

MATERIALS
Tape measure
Florist wire
Floral tape
Myrtle wire
Floral scissors
Wire cutters
Silk ribbon

FLOWERS/FOLIAGE
Clove pink
Great masterwort
Pistacia
Sea holly

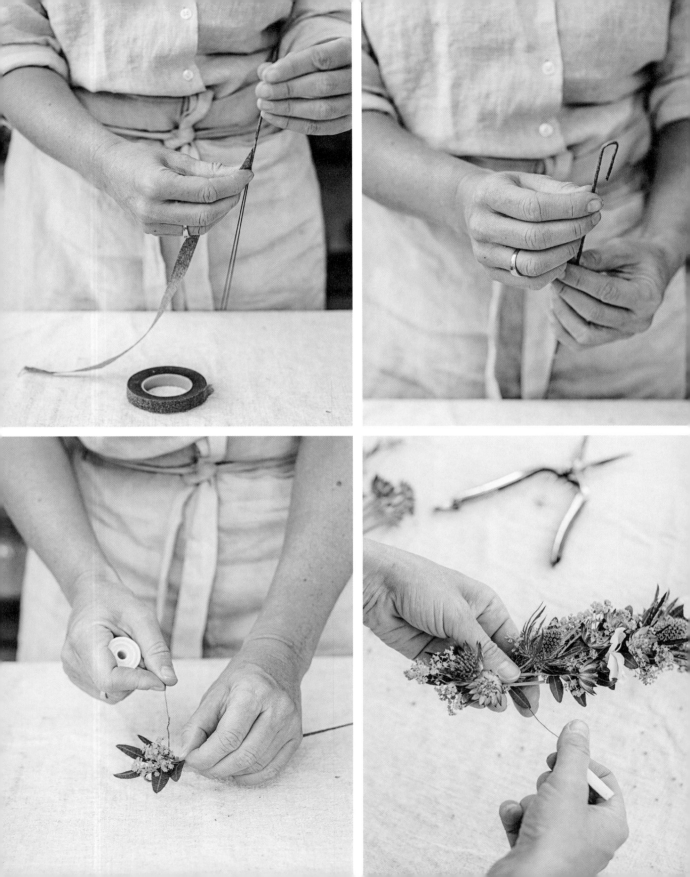

Flower crown alternative

Children are usually not that keen to wear flower crowns. Small children in particular will often pull off the flower crown as soon as it has been put on. But occasionally, us adults think that they would look so lovely with a few flowers in their hair. My solution is to add small flowers to a plastic headband. A headband will sit in place better and won't slide down the same way as a full flower crown.

I don't use large flowers, only little ones, like broad-leaved statice or baby's breath. These flowers are also very durable, which reduces the risk of the child breaking them.

LEVEL: MEDIUM

1 Cut broad-leaved statice into very small pieces.

2 Attach the myrtle wire to the headband by wrapping it around and then twisting the end.

3 Place small bunches of flowers on the headband and secure in place with the myrtle wire. You don't have to add flowers to the part of the headband that is sitting against the hair, just to the top of the band.

4 Place the next bunch of flowers over the stems of the previous ones to hide them. Make sure your bunches of flowers aren't too large, otherwise the headband will become heavy and bulky.

5 Continue the same way around the headband.

6 When you reach the end of the headband or the section you are covering, turn the final bunch of flowers the other way to hide the stems of the previous bunch.

7 Turn the headband over, cut the wire and secure in place by 'sewing' a couple of stitches into the wrapped wire.

MATERIALS
Secateurs
Myrtle wire, green
Plastic headband
Wire cutters

FLOWERS/FOLIAGE
Broad-leaved statice

Table maypole

Midsummer is a truly wonderful time, when nature is so fantastically delicate. I love a nice table setting for all seasons, and midsummer is no exception. Lovely bouquets of summer flowers like cornflower, lady's mantle and great masterwort are very welcome decorations on my table. This maypole design makes the table setting feel complete. Try to make it in a pot that's not too big, so that everything can fit comfortably on the table. I try to leave the flowers and leaves to soak up water properly before I make my wreath.

LEVEL: MEDIUM

1 Pack topsoil densely into your pot and insert a stick in the middle. Hide the soil with decorative pebbles.

2 Decorate the stick with birch branches. Attach myrtle wire and wrap it around the stick to hold the birch branches in place.

3 Bend some more birch branches into a wreath shape and join the ends together with myrtle wire. It doesn't matter if it feels a bit flimsy at the moment, it will become sturdier in the next few steps.

4 Cut the flowers into small bunches.

5 Add the flowers to the birch branch wreath, then wrap myrtle wire a couple of times around the stems to secure the flowers in place.

6 Place the next bunch of flowers on top of the stems to hide them, then secure in place with wire.

7 Repeat around the whole wreath.

8 When you reach the end, lift the first bunch of flowers and tuck the stems under to hide them.

9 Secure the myrtle wire at the back by 'sewing' a couple of stitches into the wrapped wire.

10 Tie two ribbons to four points on the wreath, opposite each other so that they cross in the middle.

11 Place the ribbons on top of the stick, secure in place with a pin or some glue, then cover with birch branches.

MATERIALS
Topsoil
Pot
Stick
Decorative pebbles
Myrtle wire, green
Floral scissors
Ribbon
Pin or glue

FLOWERS/FOLIAGE
Birch branches
Chrysanthemum
Cornflower
Lady's mantle

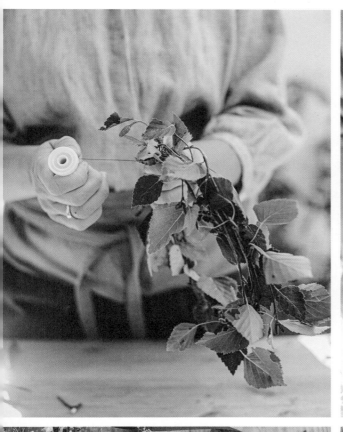

Sunny wreath with buttercups

When the meadow buttercups flower, early summer is at its finest.
I picked the flowers in this picture by the roadside in the summer rain,
with my yellow raincoat on. Buttercups dry nicely and retain their colour
for a long time, which might be hard to believe as they feel so delicate.
Together with grass, they really convey the feeling of Swedish summer.

LEVEL: MEDIUM

1 Start by wrapping a metal ring with floral tape. Secure the tape and
pull it lightly so that it gets tacky and sticks to the ring. Wrap around the
whole ring to prevent the flowers from sliding around.

2 Attach myrtle wire to the ring by wrapping it around and twisting the
end.

3 Place grass around the ring to make it thicker and hide the base, then
secure in place with myrtle wire.

4 Place a bouquet of meadow buttercups and grass on the wreath and
secure by wrapping with myrtle wire a couple of times around the stems.

5 Continue adding material around the whole wreath, placing flowers over
the stems of the previous bunches to hide them.

6 Lift the first bunch of flowers and tuck the stems under.

7 Turn the wreath over and cut the wire with wire cutters. Secure by
'sewing' a couple of stitches into the wrapped wire.

MATERIALS
Metal ring
Floral tape
Myrtle wire, green
String
Wire cutters

FLOWERS/FOLIAGE
Grass
Meadow buttercups

Bushy baby's breath

Fluffy, gorgeous baby's breath becomes a delicate summer wreath on the wall in my greenhouse. I love how bushy and playful this wreath is. Here, baby's breath gets to take centre stage, instead of being a complement to other flowers as it usually is.

LEVEL: MEDIUM

1 Start by wrapping a metal ring with floral tape. Secure the tape and pull it lightly so that it gets tacky and sticks to the ring. Wrap around the whole ring to prevent the flowers from sliding around.

2 Attach myrtle wire by wrapping it around the ring and twisting the end.

3 Cut the baby's breath into small bunches.

4 Place the flowers onto the ring and secure in place by wrapping the stems with myrtle wire.

5 Vary the length of the baby's breath to get a bushy wreath.

6 Place each bunch of flowers over the stems of the previous bunch, to hide them.

7 Continue placing baby's breath around the whole wreath.

8 Lift the first bunch of flowers so that you can tuck the stems under.

9 Turn the wreath over and cut the wire with wire cutters. Secure by 'sewing' a couple of stitches into the wrapped wire.

MATERIALS
Metal ring
Myrtle wire, green
Floral scissors
Wire cutters

FLOWERS/FOLIAGE
Baby's breath

FACT FILE DURABILITY

How long a wreath will last depends on many different factors: what time of year it is, where it is placed and, above all, which materials are used.

INDOOR WREATHS

There aren't many wreath materials that like dry, warm indoor air without water. Most materials will dry out and turn brown fairly quickly. It is possible to prolong the durability by spraying the wreath lightly with water, or placing it somewhere cool during the night.

Different kinds of moss work well indoors. Moss will dry out, but if you spray it with a little water, it will stay nice.

Eucalyptus is a favourite that dries nicely and retain its colour when dried. The same goes for other flowers that are used in dried flower arrangements, and some kinds of hydrangea.

Wreaths made from common box and broad-leaved statice also work well, but the downside is that they don't smell very nice and are therefore not particularly suitable for keeping indoors. An alternative is large-leaf box, which doesn't have any unpleasant smell.

OUTDOOR WREATHS

During the cooler part of the year, most wreaths will keep well outdoors. Many materials will dry out, but will not change much despite this. The sun can be an enemy to wreaths; they will keep better in less sunny spots. The materials that are used during the cooler period also keep better, and evergreen plants, such as conifers and ivy, will keep well without water.

In the summer it is more difficult to find materials that will keep nicely, but some herbs and lavender, for example, are able to take the heat well. Wreaths that are designed so that the plants can still get water are preferable during this time. I put flowers into test tubes filled with water, for example, or keep them in a circle-shaped vase or in a bird bath.

FLOWER CROWNS

Wreaths for the summer's festivities are often fairly short-lived, as they are only made to last for a day. I try to choose flowers that are a little bit hardier, such as chrysanthemum and carnations. It's also important to make sure that all flowers are put into water to soak properly for at least a couple of hours, preferably overnight, before the flower crown is made.

It's perfectly fine to make a flower crown the day before a summer party. Place the wreath in a plastic bag, spray water into the bag, close it and place in the fridge. The flowers will soak up the humidity from the bag and will stay nice and fresh. Take the wreath out in advance and carefully dab with kitchen roll before using.

WREATH MATERIALS

I associate early summer heavily with wreaths for midsummer and other summer parties. There's something special about beautiful flower crowns, but it can be difficult to find flowers that can go without water for a whole day. I tend to choose flowers such as cornflower, sea holly, chrysanthemum, floribunda roses or carnations. I usually combine these with a smaller flower – such as baby's breath, lady's mantle or broad-leaved statice – as well as something green, like butcher's broom or pistacia. All of these flowers usually keep well, as long as they have been left to soak up water properly before the wreaths are made (see page 82).

Baby's breath is available to buy all year round, but can also be grown in the garden. The flower is perfect to use in many wreaths since it's a nice filler. It works just as well together with other flowers as it does on its own in a white, fluffy wreath (see page 78).

In nature, there are many varieties of grass that can be nice to use at this time of year. They are at their best before midsummer; later in the season their stems can become quite hard and lose their pretty green colour.

I pick delicate meadow buttercups on my walks, and the flowers dry beautifully in my wreaths.

Broad-leaved statice and wavyleaf sea lavender are available to buy all year round and are beautiful and durable. They often retain their colour after they have dried.

I like to use green materials for wreaths that I then complement with a few flowers. In the garden, I pick ivy and box that are joined by bought branches of butcher's broom, shallon and pistacia. They all keep well and dry nicely.

Roses also dry beautifully; even if their colours fade a little when dried, they are nice to use in wreaths. Pick them before they have reached full bloom, as later on they will become more fragile and drop their petals more easily.

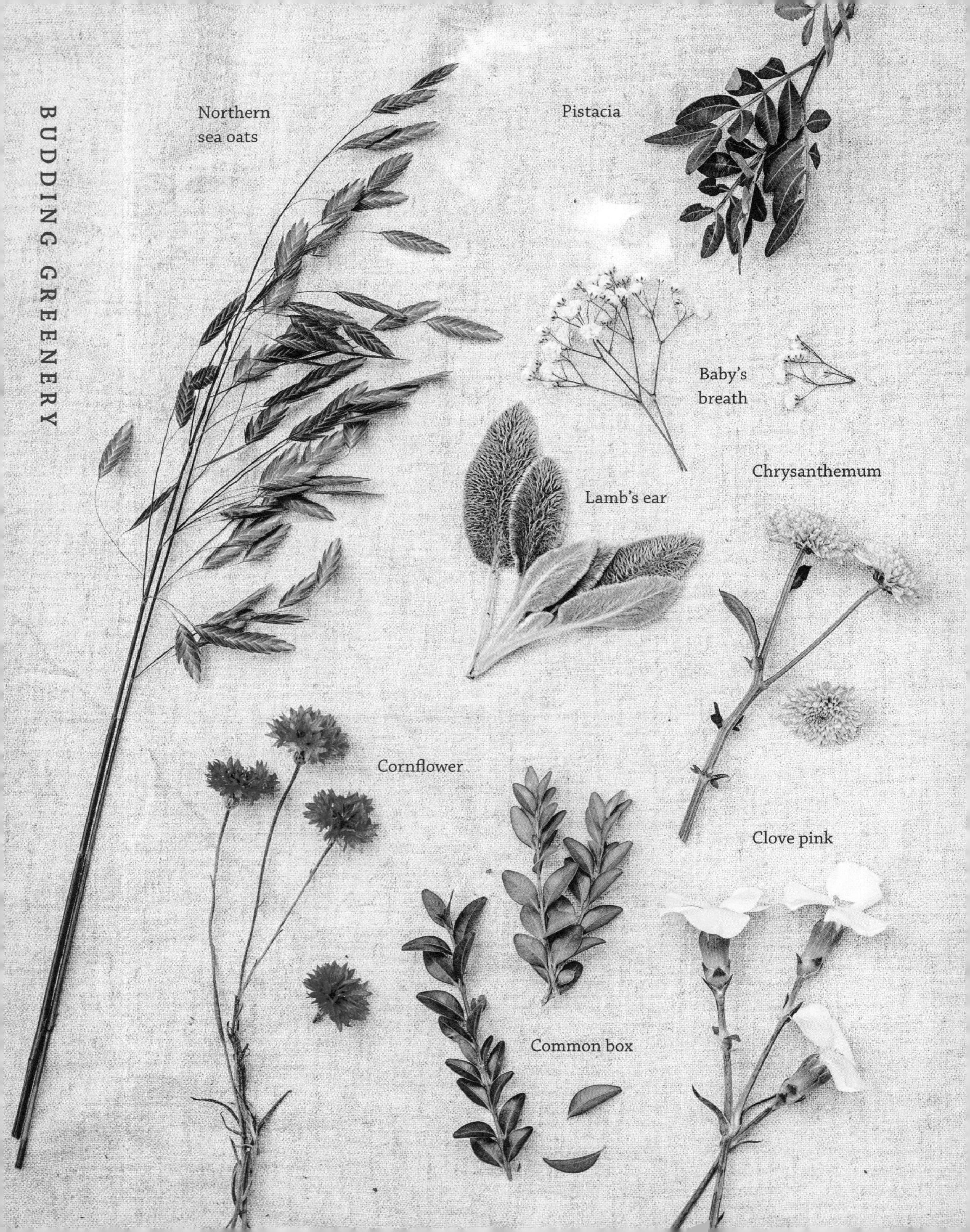

Northern
sea oats

Pistacia

Baby's
breath

Chrysanthemum

Lamb's ear

Cornflower

Clove pink

Common box

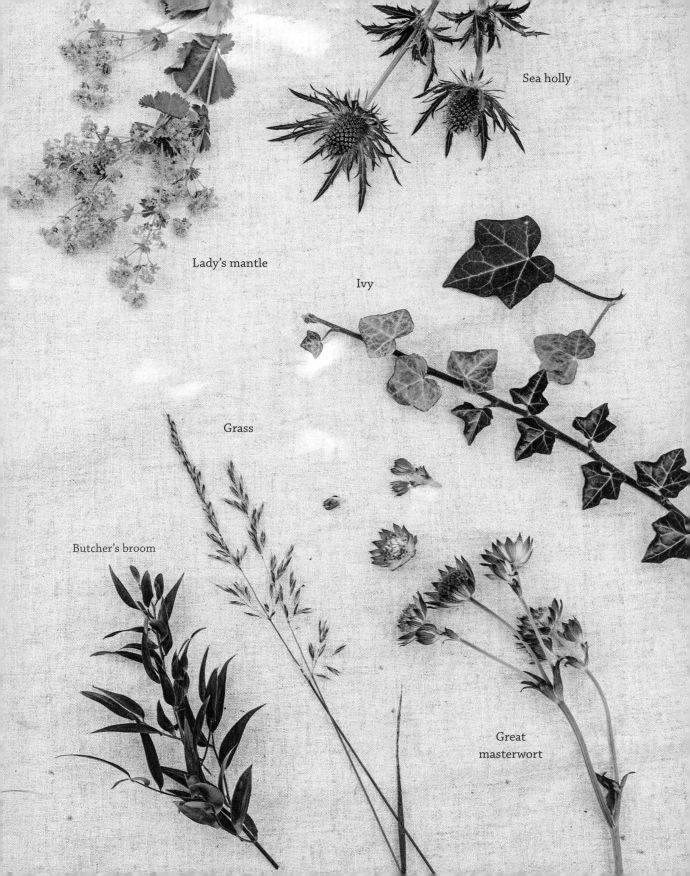

Sea holly

Lady's mantle

Ivy

Grass

Butcher's broom

Great
masterwort

Summer light

SUMMERTIME, WHEN THE DAYS are long and Öland shows its best side. Lazy days by the sea turn into warm summer evenings on the terrace.

I sneak out with bare feet early in the morning with a cup of tea and soak up the warm rays from the morning sun. I sit there for a long while and enjoy the sense of calm.

In my garden, the perennials have come up and they fill the beds beautifully. There are many green leaves in different shapes.

The pots are filled with summer flowers that add a little extra something to the garden. The agapanthus shines blue against the gravelled garden paths. In my planters, the dahlias have started to bud and the herbs are thriving in the sunshine.

The lavender is flowering and spreads a lovely scent throughout the garden. It thrives in our warm, dry soil. I cut off a few sprigs and use them in a fragrant wreath.

We enjoy a moment in the garden's sunniest spot outside the greenhouse.

Inside the greenhouse, the geraniums thrive in the heat and spread their wonderful scent. In the evenings, we come in here and get cosy on the sofa by candlelight.

I dig new beds that I fill with wonderful plants. I start different projects in every corner of the garden. I cut bouquets for summer table settings, mixing flowers from my own plants with wildflowers.

We take the picnic basket when we go for a ride around the island and visit our favourite spots. We visit beaches that aren't too crowded and cosy cafés. We spend time with friends and family who come to visit, go out on the boat and have barbecues.

Before the sun has set completely, I take a walk around the garden, water the pots and enjoy the stillness. This is my time of the day.

Dahlia birdbath

When the dahlias flower in abundance, I enjoy being able to fill the house with beautiful bouquets. Dahlias are easy to use in bouquets and come in many different shapes and pretty colours. Often, they have short stems, which I make the most of by making decorative arrangements in the garden. They keep for a long time outside and I enjoy seeing the colourful birdbath.

LEVEL: EASY

1 Cut a piece of chicken wire mesh that is long enough to turn into a ring for the bird bath.

2 Roll the chicken wire mesh into a long sausage shape.

3 Shape into a ring and squeeze the ends together. They are sharp, so should easily attach to each other.

4 Place the ring in the birdbath.

5 Cut dahlias with short stems with a knife or floral scissors. It helps to choose a variety of colours and sizes, to fill out the wreath.

6 Place the flowers into the ring until they cover the mesh completely.

7 Change the water often and the flowers should keep well.

MATERIALS
Chicken wire mesh
Secateurs/wire cutters
Knife/floral scissors
Birdbath

FLOWERS/FOLIAGE
Dahlias

Grey-green candle wreath

Our front garden gets full sun for the majority of the day during the summer. Because of this, it can be difficult to find plants that thrive there. Lamb's ear is easy to grow and thrives perfectly well in the barren soil. The soft leaves have such a nice grey-green colour and are perfect for this elegant wreath.

LEVEL: MEDIUM

1 Wrap lamb's ear around the straw base so that the leaves meet each other at the top. Secure in place with a pin.

2 Place leaves starting from the bottom of the wreath to the middle of the outside, in between the previous leaves.

3 Place leaves starting from the inside that meet the leaves from the outside to hide the top of the straw base. Make sure that the base is completely covered.

4 Insert straws of northern sea oats and broad-leaved statice under the leaves in a small section of the wreath (about a third). If needed, secure in place with more pins.

5 Place candle holders onto the base to finish.

MATERIALS
Straw base
Pins
Candle holders

FLOWERS/FOLIAGE
Broad-leaved statice
Lamb's ear
Northern sea oats

Fragrant wreath

I pass the flowering lavender, run my hand over it and smell how the fragrance fills the warm summer air. Outside my greenhouse, which gets full sun all day long during the summer, the lavender thrives. I keep potted rosemary all year round and I like to cut off sprigs both for decoration and for cooking. Together with the purple lavender, this wreath becomes an explosion of fragrance.

LEVEL: MEDIUM

1 Shape aluminium wire into a ring of your desired size.

2 Wrap the ring with floral tape, pulling the tape lightly so that it gets tacky and sticks to the ring.

3 Attach myrtle wire to the ring by wrapping it around and twisting the end to secure.

4 Start placing lavender and rosemary onto the ring. Secure in place by wrapping myrtle wire around the stems.

5 Place the next bunch over the stems of the previous bunch to hide them.

6 Continue placing material to cover the whole wreath.

7 When you reach the end, lift up the first bunch and tuck the stems under.

8 Turn the wreath over and cut the wire with wire cutters. Secure by 'sewing' a couple of stitches into the wrapped wire.

MATERIALS
Aluminium wire
Floral tape
Myrtle wire
Wire cutters

FLOWERS/FOLIAGE
Lavender
Rosemary

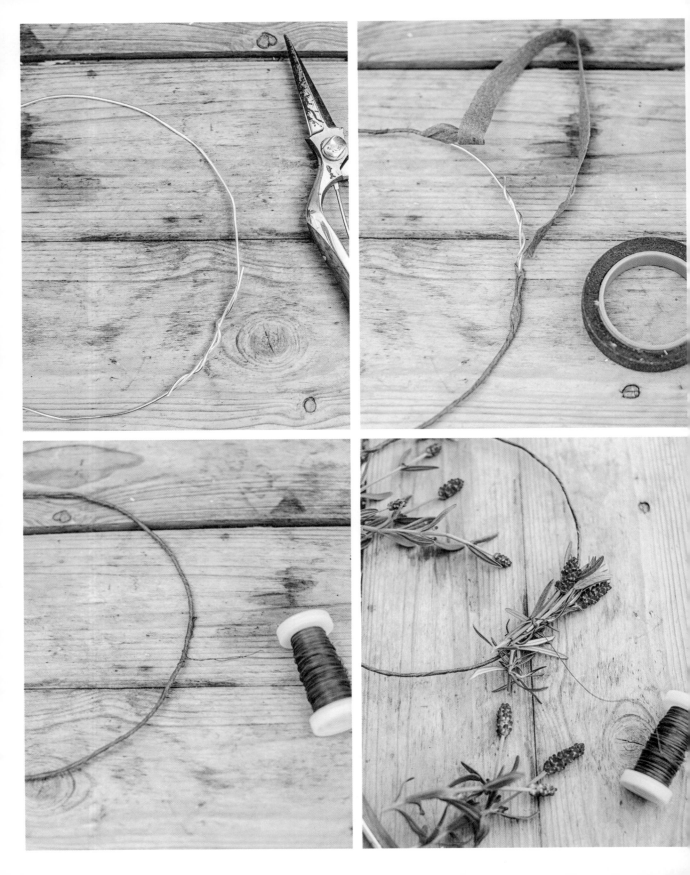

Ring of sweet peas

I sneak out in bare feet one early summer morning and feel how the sun warms the air and dries up the night's dew. Then I cut little flowers for the vase on the dining table. The fragrance fills the house as I drink my first cup of tea of the day in the morning light.

Few flowers are as lovely or give as much enjoyment as wonderfully scented, delicate sweat peas. With little maintenance they flower all summer long: the more you pick, the more flowers they produce. They work well in bouquets alongside summer flowers, but sometimes they can be more visible and take centre stage. In this decoration, they are supported by simple spiky fescue, which adds structure and form.

MATERIALS
Circle shaped vase
Knife/floral scissors

FLOWERS/FOLIAGE
Spiky fescue
Sweet pea

LEVEL: MEDIUM

1 Fill the vase with water.

2 Cut off the hard, white part of the spiky fescue.

3 Place the spiky fescue in arch shapes in between the vase openings. Make a mix of small arches (in adjacent openings) and larger arches (leaving one opening in between).

4 Let the spiky fescue form a pattern around the wreath. It can look nice when they cross over each other.

5 Give the sweet peas a fresh cut with a knife or floral scissors before you place them in the vase. Use the spiky fescue as a support when you insert the flowers into the vase.

6 Let the shape of the flowers direct and follow the shape of the wreath.

7 Place flowers both above the spiky fescue and further down in the vase to create some variety.

Tall summer flowers

In my planters, lovely summer flowers like snapdragon and garden cosmos are growing. The coriander has started to bloom and is so incredibly delicate and beautiful.

I love using flowering herbs in my floral works. They are pretty in their form and add such a wonderful fragrance. In a decoration with height, the snapdragon is allowed to shine and be properly visible.

LEVEL: EASY

1 Place the flower frog in a cylindrical bowl with fresh water.

2 Place snapdragon around the ring at different heights.

3 Arrange garden cosmos in the same way.

4 Finish the arrangement with coriander flowers around the whole ring.

MATERIALS
**Ring-shaped
  flower frog
Cylindrical bowl**

FLOWERS/FOLIAGE
**Coriander in bloom
Garden cosmos
Snapdragon**

Cereal and flax wreath

It is a warm summer evening and the cereal crops are swaying in the sun.
I take a walk past the fields and listen to them rustling in the wind. I make
a wreath from oat, wheat and flax before the grains have ripened. I am
reminded that summer is coming to an end and that harvest time is near.

LEVEL: MEDIUM

1 Start by attaching the reel wire to the straw base by wrapping it around
and twisting the end to secure it.

2 Place bunches of oat onto the wreath and secure in place by wrapping the
reel wire around the stems.

3 Continue arranging the oat so that the whole wreath is covered.

4 Follow the same steps with the wheat and flax, using each bunch to
cover the stems of the previous bunches.

5 When you reach the end, lift up the first bunch and tuck the stems
under to keep them hidden.

6 Turn the wreath over and cut the wire with wire cutters. Secure by
'sewing' a couple of stitches into the wrapped wire. Push the sharp end
into the wreath to keep it in place.

MATERIALS
Reel wire
Straw base
Floral scissors
Secateurs
Wire cutters

FLOWERS/FOLIAGE
Flax
Oat
Wheat

Roadside flower wreath

During late summer, the wildflowers usually get fewer and fewer here on Öland, due to the drought. After weeks of sun and minimal rainfall there isn't much that still manages to grow.

Weeds such as curly dock are hardy and I like to use them in bouquets. Here, they are given prime position together with tansy, which also defies the climate and keeps flowering faithfully.

LEVEL: MEDIUM

1 Start by wrapping a metal ring with floral tape. Secure the tape and pull it lightly so that it gets tacky and sticks to the ring. Wrap around the whole ring to prevent the flowers from sliding around.

2 Attach myrtle wire to the ring by wrapping the wire around it and twisting the end.

3 Start by adding tansy to the wreath, securing in place with the wire.

4 Continue with curly dock the same way. Place each bunch of flowers over the stems of the previous bunch to cover them.

5 Keep adding flowers until the whole wreath is covered.

6 When you reach the end, lift up the first bunch of flowers and tuck the stems under.

7 Turn the wreath over and cut the wire with wire cutters. Secure by 'sewing' a couple of stitches into the wrapped wire.

MATERIALS
Metal ring
Floral tape
Myrtle wire, green
Wire cutters

FLOWERS/FOLIAGE
Curly dock
Tansy

FACT FILE PICKED AND BOUGHT

PICKED

I love using flowers and plants from nature or the garden in my flower decorations, so I always have secateurs or a knife to hand. You never know what pretty things you might come across.

Sometimes I walk past a nice garden with beautiful things growing in it and I ask if I can take a small branch. I'm almost always allowed; often people are pleased to hear that I think they have a nice garden.

When I pick flowers or branches, I carry a bucket of water with me, so I can place them directly in there. This helps to keep them fresh. When I come home with my finds, I then give them a fresh cut.

What are you allowed to pick in nature? This can be quite a tricky subject, and laws vary from place to place. Generally, you are able to pick wildflowers that are not critically endangered or privately owned. But you're not allowed to dig up plants or pick them in a way that will damage them, and sometimes you will need permission from the landowner. As a general rule, you should pick only 1 flower from a patch of 20 – and it's best to leave them alone if there are fewer than 20. You are usually allowed to pick up dry twigs, branches and cones from the ground, but you cannot break or saw off branches from trees.

Some plants are protected, which in most cases means that you're not allowed to pick them. This is even the case if the plant grows on your own land. Some protected plants cannot be picked at all. In other cases, protection of a plant can mean that you're allowed to pick a bouquet for yourself, but that digging them up by the roots or picking them to sell for profit is prohibited. A plant that is protected in one area doesn't necessarily have to be protected in other areas, so it's best to check before picking any plant or flower.

BOUGHT

Of course, not all materials are possible to find in nature, and at some times of the year there isn't much growing in the garden. In this case, I supplement with flowers and plant material bought from the shops.

Nowadays, flowers are sold in many shops that also sell other products. I recommend that you buy flowers and plant materials from your local florist or garden centre. They have competent staff who take care of the flowers the right way, so that they're in good condition when you bring them home.

Always buy flowers that look fresh. If you give them a squeeze, they should feel hard. When you come home with your flowers, give them a fresh cut and place them in water in a cool place. Make sure they get to soak up water properly before you start using them in wreaths or arrangements. Change the water often and give the flowers new cuts every now and then; this will prolong their life by several days.

Most flowers and plants prefer cooler temperatures, so one tip to make them last longer is to place them in the fridge or another cool place during the night.

WREATH MATERIALS

The summer is the most difficult time to get hold of material for wreaths. There isn't much material that can last without water in the sun and the heat. Therefore, I try to make wreaths where the flowers can access water. There are many lovely summer flowers to use, such as sweet pea, dahlia and snapdragon.

Lavender, however, is a flower that dries beautifully and is perfect to use in wreaths without water (see page 98). In my dry beds, the lavender thrives. I cut the flowers before they have fully blossomed, when they are at their most beautiful.

In my herb beds, herbs flourish during this season, and most herbs dry nicely: rosemary, thyme, oregano and sage are great in a wreath.

In late summer, there are many flowers and plants that will dry beautifully. Flax and cereal grass are lovely in wreaths (see page 113) – and the wreaths will last for ages. Then they can become food for garden birds in winter.

Broad-leaved statice and wavyleaf sea lavender always dry beautifully and will retain their colour well.

Many seed pods work well in wreaths, for example scabiosa and clematis.

Evergreen plants, such as common box and ivy, are favourites and I use them in lots of summer wreaths. The leaves from coral bells also dry nicely and their different colours look so beautiful.

Bought materials, such as butcher's broom, pistacia and shallon, are all hardy and work perfectly for green wreaths.

Roadside flowers, such as tansy, dry nicely – they are wonderful in summer wreaths. Grasses are still nice too, even though they change colour slightly in the summer. The grasses in my garden have started to come up with beautiful flower heads that I cut for wreaths.

Flowers such as globe thistle and sea holly both dry nicely and I like to use both of these in my summer wreaths.

In the south-facing front garden of my house, lamb's ear flourishes. I love using these leaves: they dry nicely and have a lovely grey-green colour (see page 95).

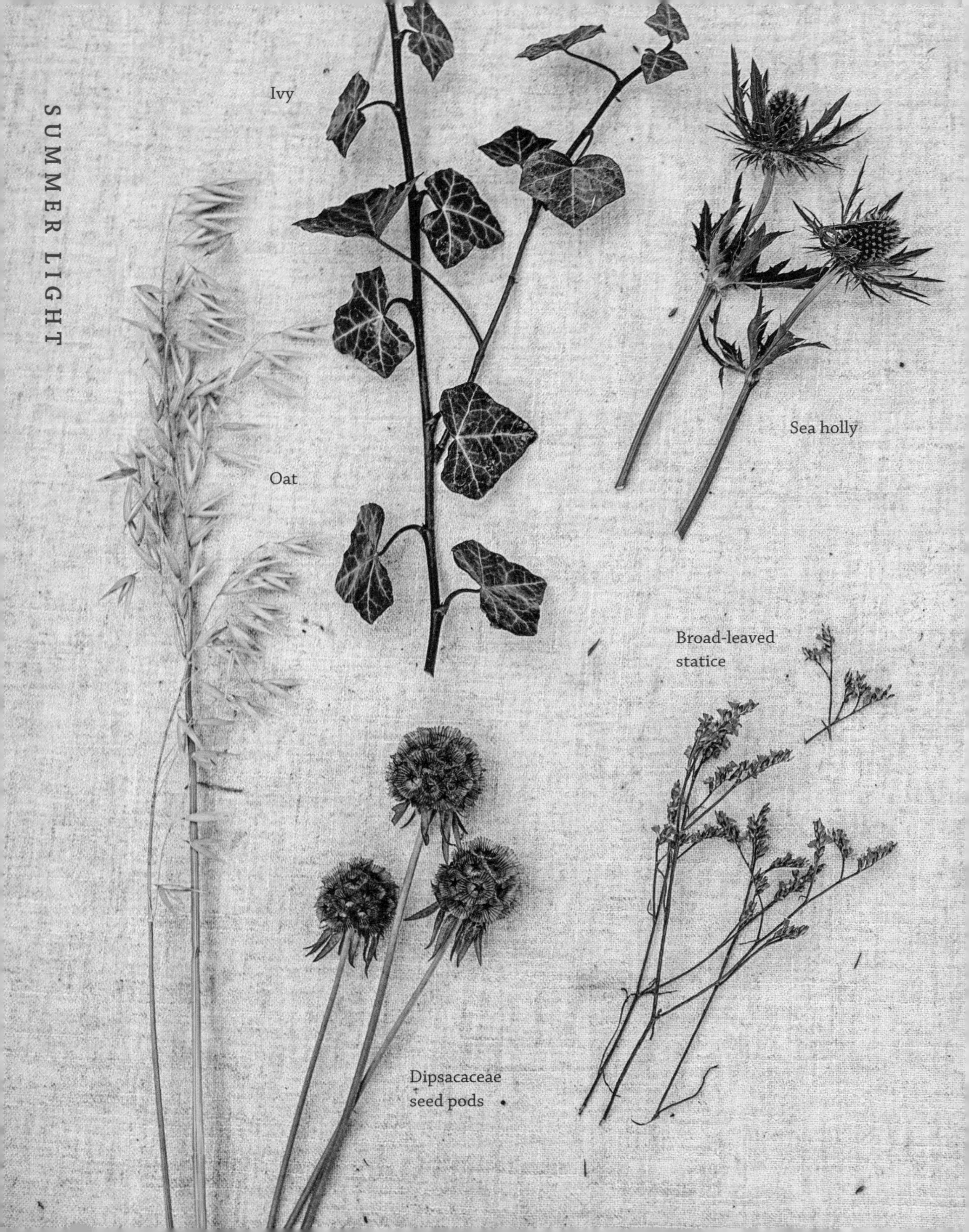

Ivy

Sea holly

Oat

Broad-leaved
statice

Dipsacaceae
seed pods •

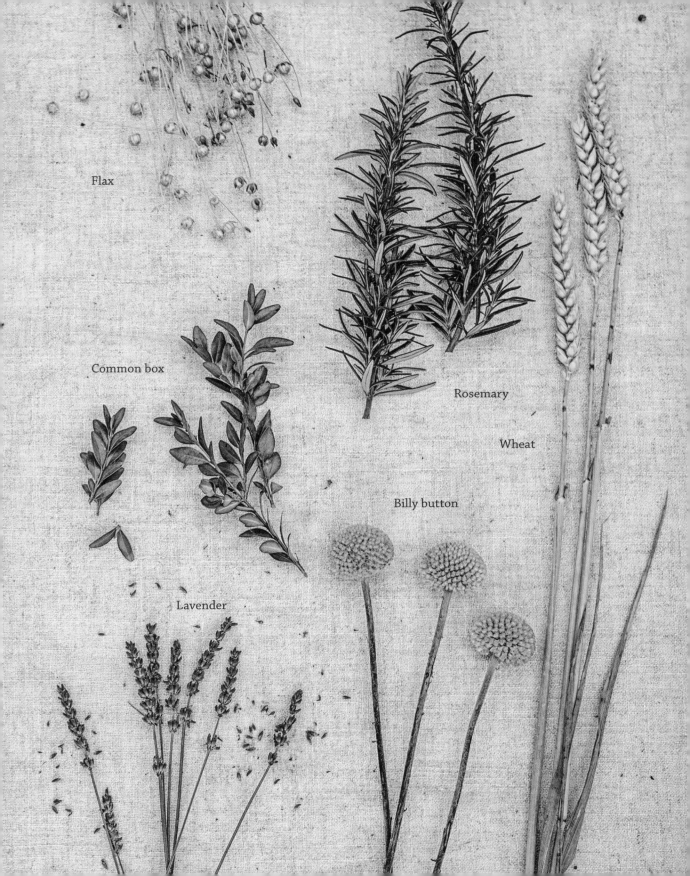

Flax

Common box

Rosemary

Wheat

Billy button

Lavender

Harvest time

WHEN SUMMER IS COMING to an end and the light turns golden, I enjoy our colour-sparkling nature. The colours on the trees and shrubs give us a last treat before it's time for winter's rest. I catch the Japanese maple in its full glory before the red leaves carpet the path, together with the katsura tree's yellow gingerbread-scented leaves. Fallen leaves from oak and maple trees become beautiful decorations, both inside and outside.

In the glade, the ferns stand high with golden leaves, and by the sea the reeds sway beautifully. I collect a handful for the house. I pick berries and make lovely hydrangea wreaths.

The dahlias are still in bloom and the last bouquets are brought in to decorate the kitchen table. It's high time to make the most of the summer's harvest. Herbs are frozen, and at my local farmer's market, I buy vegetables that I preserve for winter.

Flowers are hung out to dry to be used for winter's wreaths, when the offering from the garden is more limited. I cut beautiful seed pods and place them in vases.

I enjoy the calm that arrives on the island. The fields are now filled with pumpkins in different shapes and colours. I take some home with me and place them in the garden alongside pots in autumnal colours. Summer flowers are replaced by heather, cushion bush and skimmia.

Still, the sun's rays are warm and I soak up all the light that I can. I enjoy cleaning up the garden, raking leaves and removing fallen branches. Plants I haven't had time to do anything with are dug into the ground. I cross my fingers hoping they will survive the winter. Some bulbs are planted in beds and pots, with the hope of beautiful blooming in spring.

In the greenhouse, the geraniums stand big and beautiful. I leave them in here for as long as I can, then I will put them away and bring them back again in the spring. We enjoy brunch in the greenhouse and soak up the last of the season.

A desire for decorating indoors and creating a cosy space slowly sets in. It's time to move indoors again, light candles and get under a blanket. It's a nice time.

Autumn wreath with a dash of blue

Autumn is a wonderfully colourful time. When nature explodes with colour, I want my wreaths to mirror this. The blue of the sky and the sea together with orange and brown tones complete a picture of nature on a sunny autumn day.

I like to pick berries and leaves, both in the garden and when I'm out on my autumn walks, and mix them with a few bought sprigs.

MATERIALS
Secateurs
Myrtle wire, green
Wire cutters
Jute twine

FLOWERS/FOLIAGE
Chinese lantern
English yew
Eucalyptus
Fern
Grass
Oak leaves
Pink pepper berries
Rosehips
Sea holly
Virginia creeper

LEVEL: ADVANCED

1 Remove the leaves from the Virginia creeper vines.

2 Shape the vines into a ring and twist them together.

3 Continue adding to the ring and make it sturdier by wrapping more vines around it.

4 Attach the myrtle wire by wrapping it around the base and twisting the end.

5 Start adding sea holly to the wreath, wrapping the myrtle wire around the stems.

6 Continue with the other materials. Place each bunch of material over the stems of the previous bunch to hide them.

7 Add material to cover roughly one-third of the base.

8 Cut the myrtle wire with wire cutters, then secure the wire at the back by 'sewing' a couple of stitches into the wrapped wire.

9 Attach some more myrtle wire on the opposite side of the wreath from the first bunch of sea holly.

10 Place sea holly facing the other way and secure in place with myrtle wire.

11 Repeat steps 5–8, so that the two sides of the wreath almost meet in the middle.

12 Tie jute twine over the stems. Wrap the twine tightly over the ends of the stems and moving slightly upwards over the base. Repeat on the opposite side to finish.

Asymmetry with ferns

In the forest, the ferns grow high. Their golden tones glitter in autumn's soft sunrays. I pick some and make them into wreaths that dry beautifully. The brown colour of the ferns is a nice contrast against the blue-green colour of the eucalyptus. A few berries act as an extra eye-catcher, and the grasses contribute a softer material.

LEVEL: ADVANCED

1 Attach myrtle wire to the base by wrapping the wire around it and twisting the end.

2 Start adding fern to the base, securing it in place by wrapping myrtle wire around the stem a couple of times.

3 Continue with the eucalyptus and grass, securing them in the same way as above.

4 Mix in some Swedish whitebeam berries in a few places.

5 Add plant material to two thirds of the wreath base.

6 Cut the myrtle wire with wire cutters, then turn the wreath over and secure to the back by 'sewing' a couple of stitches into the wrapped wire.

7 Hide the stems at the end with hessian ribbon, leaving it to hang down a little for extra decoration.

MATERIALS
Base made from branches
Myrtle wire, green
Wire cutters
Hessian ribbon

FLOWERS/FOLIAGE
Eucalyptus nicholii
Fern
Grass
Swedish whitebeam berries (or other colourful berries)

Dense wreath with strawflower

I like to pick strawflowers in the summer and dry them for using in wreaths in the autumn and winter. These wonderful flowers retain their colour just as well even after they have dried. I mix them with beautiful hydrangea, berries and autumnal leaves to create a wreath that stays nice for a long time.

Bushy broad-leaved statice and dried grass provide great contrast, both in colour and shape.

LEVEL: MEDIUM

1 Start by wrapping a metal ring with floral tape. Secure the tape and pull it lightly so that it gets tacky and sticks to the ring. Wrap around the whole ring to prevent the flowers from sliding around.

2 Attach myrtle wire to the ring by wrapping it all the way around and twisting the end.

3 Start adding broad-leaved statice to the ring, securing it in place by wrapping the wire around the stems.

4 Add florets of hydrangea, pressing the flowers together and securing with myrtle wire.

5 Continue varying other plants and flowers around the ring, densely filling the whole wreath.

6 Lift the first bunch of broad-leaved statice and tuck the stems under so they are hidden.

7 Turn the wreath over and cut the wire with wire cutters. Secure by 'sewing' a couple of stitches into the wrapped wire.

MATERIALS
Metal ring
Floral tape
Myrtle wire, green
Secateurs
Wire cutters

FLOWERS/FOLIAGE
Broad-leaved statice
Eucalyptus
Hydrangea
Oak leaves
Phalaris
Rosehips
Strawflower

Rosy hydrangea wreath with blackberries

When summer starts to turn into autumn, I pick beautiful blackberries on my walks. They are thorny, but oh so beautiful.

Lovely hydrangea blooms that, just like nature, shift from green to rusty tones, are hard to resist. This wreath makes the most of useful and durable hydrangea, as well as heather for added bushiness. It is a wreath that dries beautifully, so you can enjoy it all autumn long.

LEVEL: MEDIUM

1 Start by wrapping the metal ring with floral tape to prevent the flowers from sliding around. Secure the tape and pull it lightly so that it gets tacky. Wrap the tape around the whole wreath.

2 Attach myrtle wire to the ring by wrapping it around and then twisting the end.

3 Using secateurs, cut a heather plant into smaller pieces.

4 Start adding heather to the wreath, placing a small bunch and wrapping myrtle wire around the stems to keep it place.

5 Divide the hydrangea using your secateurs and take a small part of it. Pack the flowers tightly together, as they will shrink as they dry. Place the hydrangea over the stems of the heather and wrap myrtle wire around it to secure it in place.

6 Continue the same way with the blackberries, cutting them into smaller bunches.

7 Repeat around the whole wreath, placing each bunch of flowers so that it covers the stems of the previous bunch.

8 When you reach the end of the wreath, lift up the first bunch of heather and tuck the stems under.

9 Turn the wreath over and cut the wire with wire cutters. Secure by 'sewing' a couple of stitches into the wrapped wire.

MATERIALS
Metal ring
Floral tape
Myrtle wire, green
Secateurs
Wire cutters

FLOWERS/FOLIAGE
Heather
Hydrangea
Blackberries

Green autumn wreath

On Öland, ivy grows wild everywhere. It's thriving to the extent that in many places it takes over everything and starves off the trees. I love ivy and have it in many places in my garden. Older plants change leaf shape and will grow flowers, which are loved by bees. These flowers then turn into beautiful berries later in the year.

I use the berries in decorations during autumn and winter. In this wreath I have mixed them with beautiful hop cones.

LEVEL: MEDIUM

1 Start by wrapping a metal ring with floral tape. Secure the tape and pull it lightly so that it gets tacky and sticks to the ring. Wrap around the whole ring to prevent the flowers from sliding around.

2 Attach myrtle wire to the ring by wrapping it around and then twisting the end.

3 Add bunches ivy to the ring, securing it in place by wrapping the wire around the stems.

4 Remove the leaves from the hop cones.

5 Add the cones to the ring and secure in the same way as above.

6 Repeat, adding materials around the whole wreath.

7 When you reach the end, lift up the first bunch of ivy and tuck the stems under.

8 Turn the wreath over and cut the wire with wire cutters. Secure by 'sewing' a couple of stitches into the wrapped wire.

MATERIALS
Metal ring
Floral tape
Myrtle wire, green
Wire cutters

FLOWERS/FOLIAGE
Hop cones
Ivy

Dark toned wreath

I love these magical flowers in dark tones, there's something almost surreal about them. The dark hydrangea marries so well with the orpine and the skimmia in this wreath. The rosehip gives contrast, and the cushion bush gives the wreath that little extra something.

LEVEL: MEDIUM

1 Using secateurs, cut a cushion bush plant into smaller pieces.

2 Divide the hydrangea and orpine into smaller pieces and cut the rosehip stems to a shorter length.

3 Attach the myrtle wire to the straw base by wrapping it around the base and twisting the end.

4 Take the smaller pieces of hydrangea and mix it with orpine to create a small bunch.

5 Start placing the bunches of flowers so that they cover the straw base.

6 Secure in place by wrapping myrtle wire around the stems.

7 Place the each bunch of flowers so that they cover the stems of the previous bunch.

8 Slot different kinds of rosehips into the wreath.

9 Mix in small pieces of cushion bush, skimmia and coral bells.

10 Add materials around the whole wreath.

11 When you reach the end, lift up the first bunch of flowers to tuck the stems under.

12 Turn the wreath over and cut the wire with wire cutters. Secure by 'sewing' a couple of stitches into the wrapped wire.

MATERIALS
Secateurs
Straw base
Myrtle wire, green
Wire cutters

FLOWERS/FOLIAGE
Coral bells
Cushion bush
Hydrangea
Orpine
Rosehips
Skimmia

Rosehip candle lantern wreath

Rosehips are so incredibly beautiful; it's amazing that roses can create these beautiful berries! They do have long, horrible thorns, so make sure you have a good pair of gloves on when handling them.

Usually, I use rosehips as accents in decorations, but in this wreath they get to take centre stage. With different varieties of rosehips and a bit of moss as a base, this wreath makes a lovely decoration for a candle lantern.

LEVEL: MEDIUM

1 Start by shaping aluminium wire into a suitable-sized ring and twist the ends together.

2 Wrap a metal ring with floral tape. Secure the tape and pull it lightly so that it gets tacky and sticks to the ring. Wrap around the whole ring to prevent the flowers from sliding around.

3 Attach myrtle wire to the ring by wrapping it around it and twisting the end.

4 Place moss around the ring to cover the aluminium wire, then secure in place with myrtle wire. Make sure the whole ring is covered with moss.

5 Add rosehips to the ring, securing in place by wrapping myrtle wire around the stems.

6 Continue adding different varieties of rosehips, using each bunch to cover the stems of the previous bunches to hide them.

7 When you reach the end, lift up the first bunch of rosehips to tuck the stems under.

8 Turn the wreath over and cut the wire with wire cutters. Secure by 'sewing' a couple of stitches into the wrapped wire.

MATERIALS
Aluminium wire
Floral tape
Myrtle wire, green
Wire cutters

FLOWERS/FOLIAGE
Moss
**Rosehips, different
     varieties**

Rowan wreath

Beautiful rowan berries shine brightly in the autumn sun and I pick a few berries from the lower branches. The sight of the beautiful bunches tells me that autumn is coming. In the flower bed, orpine loyally pops up every year and I cut off a few flowers for my wreath. The heather's strong pink colour really brightens up the autumn darkness and adds life to this wreath.

This wreath dries beautifully, so I can enjoy it throughout the autumn. I hang it close to the house so that no birds come and eat the berries.

LEVEL: MEDIUM

1 Cut up a few heather plants into smaller bunches using secateurs.

2 Wrap a metal ring with floral tape. Secure the tape and pull it lightly so that it gets tacky and sticks to the ring. Wrap around the whole ring to prevent the flowers from sliding around.

3 Attach the myrtle wire by wrapping it around the ring and twisting the end.

4 Start adding heather to the ring, wrapping myrtle wire around the stems to secure it in place.

5 Add bunches of rowan berries and secure them the same way.

6 Next, add the orpine. Alternate all of the plants around the whole wreath, making sure to place each bunch over the stems of the previous bunch to hide them.

7 When you reach the end, lift up the bunch of heather you started with and tuck the stems under.

8 Turn the wreath over and cut the wire with wire cutters. Secure by 'sewing' a couple of stitches into the wrapped wire.

MATERIALS
Secateurs
Metal ring
Floral tape
Myrtle wire, green
Wire cutters

FLOWERS/FOLIAGE
Heather
Orpine
Rowan berries

Lichen and strawflower wreath

As autumn comes to an end and winter approaches, a wreath with beautiful cladonia lichen and mossy sloe branches is perfect. Along the coast, there are thorny bushes of sloe that, because of the damp climate, get covered in a beautiful layer of moss. I like to pick these for my wreaths and decorations. In this wreath, sloe and cladonia lichen are accompanied by the last hydrangeas from the garden, as well as rosehips and a few dried strawflowers that brighten it up nicely.

LEVEL: MEDIUM

1 Start by wrapping a metal ring with floral tape. Secure the tape and pull it lightly so that it gets tacky and sticks to the ring. Wrap around the whole ring to prevent the flowers from sliding around.

2 Attach myrtle wire to the ring by wrapping it around and twisting the end.

3 Divide the hydrangea into smaller pieces using secateurs.

4 Add cladonia lichen to the ring and secure by wrapping myrtle wire around it a couple of times.

5 Continue adding sloe branches, hydrangea, rosehips and strawflowers to the ring. Make sure to cover the stems of the previous material so that they are hidden, then secure in place with myrtle wire.

6 Repeat around the whole ring.

7 When you reach the end, lift up the first plants you placed and tuck the stems under.

8 Turn the wreath over and cut the wire with wire cutters. Secure by 'sewing' a couple of stitches into the wrapped wire.

MATERIALS
Metal ring
Floral tape
Myrtle wire, green
Secateurs
Wire cutters

FLOWERS/FOLIAGE
Cladonia lichen
Hydrangea
Rosehips
Sloe branches
Strawflower

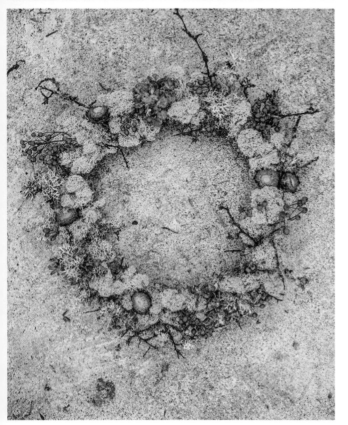

Tip!

Save your cladonia lichen from one year to the next, preferably keeping it in a shaded place during the summer months. Wet the lichen and it will become nice and soft again.

FACT FILE HOW TO CHOOSE MATERIALS

FORM

When I choose materials for my wreaths, my starting point is to consider the feeling that I want the wreath to convey.

Plants have different forms and textures that I take into consideration. Flowers and plants can be round or pointy, or they can grow in dense or bushy ways.

I often choose a main material that is used as the wreath base, preferably a material that fills the wreath out well and is calm in its form. Our eyes interpret round forms as calmer and more harmonious, whereas a wreath with only pointy forms might be regarded as messier.

I then choose material to decorate with that has a different form and structure to the main material. The materials should lift each other and come together in harmony. I often choose 1–3 complementing materials. You can of course choose more, but I prefer fewer.

When it comes to making the wreaths, I repeat the materials to create an even pattern over the whole wreath. Sometimes I deviate from this and make an asymmetrical wreath with different materials, which can also be exciting. If I want to create a wreath that gives off a calm impression, I only use one material.

COLOUR

When I choose colours for my wreaths I like to work with colours of similar hues. It's the simplest way to combine different colours together. Different shades of a colour or similar colours will always create a nice harmony.

If I wish to create a more colourful wreath, I choose colours that complement each other; that is, colours that sit opposite each other in the colour wheel, as far away from each other as possible.

The colour green can be included in all arrangements, as our eyes don't see it as its own colour in flower arrangements.

WREATH MATERIALS

Even though Advent and Christmas are often associated with wreaths, I would say that the high season for wreaths is harvest season. There is an abundance of beautiful materials to pick for wreaths at this time of the year.

Rowan berries and rosehips glow beautifully red, both on their own but also when combined with other materials. Rowan berries are among the first berries to ripen; further into autumn the berries will often become mushy. Because of this, I try to pick them as soon as they get their red colour. Elderberries also ripen early; I try to pick them when they're still green to use them while they're still nice.

Both blackberries and Swedish whitebeam berries work well in wreaths. I try to pick blackberries before they have become fully ripe, since they become soft and fragile later in the season. Swedish whitebeam berries, which we have an abundance of on Öland, ripen later in the season than rowan berries. These berries keep better than rowan berries, as they don't become as soft. I gladly add these to autumn's wreaths (see page 133).

But the prima donna of autumn is the hydrangea. Few materials are as beautiful in wreaths as this flower. I choose the flowers that shift towards green, and I have found that the pink and burgundy varieties keep the best. When I make my wreaths, I divide the big flowers and use smaller parts. Wreaths are beautiful with just hydrangea on its own, but it also works well with the season's berries and leaves (see page 142).

Coral bells and ivy are two leaf favourites at this time of the year. Both dry beautifully and make a nice contrast to other plants. I have coral bells growing both in beds and in pots. They come in a range of colours, and some have beautiful veins that are nicely visible.

In my garden, ivy grows both covering the ground and as a climber. On my old willow, it climbs far up the trunk and I often cut off stems and leaves. Older specimens of ivy will often flower in the autumn, and these look nice in wreaths. Closer to winter, the flowers turn into beautiful berries with tinges of green and black. If you don't have the benefit of finding ivy growing wild in nature or have it in your own garden, you can just as well take cuttings from your pot plants.

I like to cut heather for my wreaths. Pink cape heath keeps the best, as it doesn't change colour when dried and it also works for indoor wreaths. Other varieties tend to turn brown quite quickly.

Cushion bush plants are another firm favourite; the plant gives a bushy feel to wreaths that are otherwise neat and orderly. Its silvery colour also brightens a wreath up nicely (see page 150).

Orpine comes in many varieties and colours and all work well in wreaths and dry beautifully. I mix orpine with both hydrangea and heather.

Wilted flowers can also be nice, and many perennials get beautiful seed pods, such as echinacea and scabiosa. They look lovely in autumnal wreaths.

Blackberry

Oak

Hydrangea

Elderberry

Heather

Fern

Rosehip

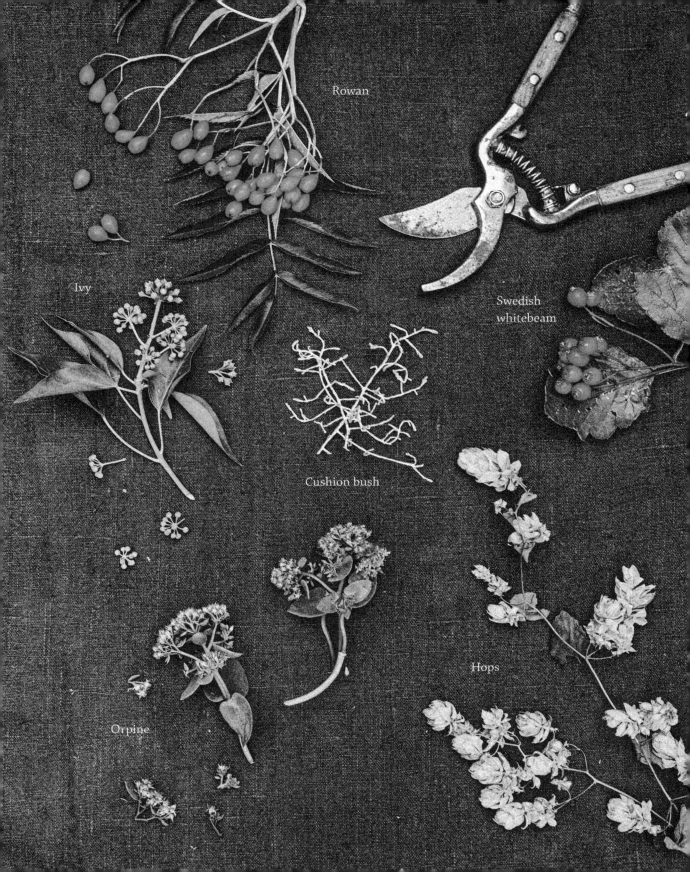

Rowan

Ivy

Swedish
whitebeam

Cushion bush

Orpine

Hops

Winter rest

THE LEAVES HAVE FALLEN to the ground and the bare branches are stretching towards the sky. On cold nights, the garden gets covered in a white, frosty blanket. My steps make a crunchy sound when I sneak out early one morning to photograph the beautiful frost that has given lace edges to all the beautiful evergreen leaves and seed pods.

The garden and nature are resting; it's both sad and a relief at the same time. We need a break from each other so that my lust for digging and planting can return in the spring.

When the days become shorter and darkness starts to arrive in the afternoon, I put up plenty of fairy lights in the garden: they light up the darker months nicely. I plant evergreen plants in pots and decorate them with moss. They will last well all winter here in our mild climate. I also lay spruce branches on the ground, decorated with fairy lights. I like to add branches of spruce and pine to pots with perennials. They serve the dual function of protecting the plants and looking decorative.

I pull on my hat and take a walk in the pine forest. Here, I pick cones and mossy sloe branches that I push into pots with hellebores. Wreaths decorate walls and tables in the garden. Around the entrance, I hang beautiful spruce garlands.

Preparing for Christmas and Advent is my favourite time of year. I love the cosiness and the warmth of this season, and Christmas music starts to fill my home from the beginning of November. The house is filled with hyacinths, branches of pine and spruce and bouquets with beautiful amaryllis. To make the season last longer, I always start decorating early so that I can enjoy this cosy time for as long as possible.

When the Öland wind is whistling around the corners of the house, I light a fire and curl up on the sofa with a cup of tea in a room lit by many candles. The house is filled with the scent of dried orange slices, cinnamon, star anise, cloves and freshly baked saffron buns.

Eucalyptus wreath

In the autumn and winter the availability of eucalyptus is at its best. I love both the colour and the form. Eucalyptus comes in many different forms, most of which have the same beautiful grey-green colour.

I usually make wreaths that I hang up in the kitchen, where I leave them to dry. They retain their colour when dried and they smell lovely. If you have your own plants, you can cut branches from them for your wreaths.

LEVEL: MEDIUM

1 Start by wrapping a metal ring with floral tape. Secure the tape and pull it lightly so that it gets tacky and sticks to the ring. Wrap around the whole ring to prevent the eucalyptus from sliding around.

2 Attach myrtle wire to the ring by wrapping it around and twisting the end to secure.

3 With secateurs, divide the eucalyptus into smaller pieces. Eucalyptus cinerea can be split between the leaf pairs, meaning you get many little branches out of it.

4 Add a couple of branches of eucalyptus cinerea to the ring and secure in place by wrapping myrtle wire around the stems a couple of times.

5 Place a bunch of eucalyptus with berries, covering the stems from the previous bunch, then secure in place with myrtle wire.

6 Alternate the two different varieties around the whole wreath.

7 When you reach the end, lift the first bunch of eucalyptus to tuck the stems under.

8 Turn the wreath over and cut the wire with wire cutters. Secure by 'sewing' a couple of stitches into the wrapped wire.

MATERIALS
Metal ring
Floral tape
Myrtle wire, green
Secateurs
Wire cutters

FLOWERS/FOLIAGE
Eucalyptus cinerea
Eucalyptus with
  berries

Bushy green wreath with larch

By the entrance to my garden, I have a black wooden fence where every year I hang large, bushy wreaths, to give a welcoming impression. In November, I hang up wreaths in different green tones. For this one, I have mixed many different materials – I let the pine stick out slightly so the wreath has a lovely, bushy appearance. The larch branches also protrude and add life to the wreath.

LEVEL: ADVANCED

1 Start by wrapping a metal ring with floral tape. Secure the tape and pull it lightly so that it gets tacky and sticks to the ring. Wrap around the whole ring to prevent the flowers from sliding around.

2 Attach myrtle wire to the ring by wrapping it around and twisting the end to secure.

3 Divide the material into smaller pieces using secateurs. The holly can be cut between the leaf pairs so that the whole branch can be used.

4 Place a couple of pine branches onto the ring and secure in place by wrapping the myrtle wire around them a couple of times.

5 Place the next bunch of pine branches so that the stems of the previous bunch are hidden, then secure with myrtle wire.

6 Mix spruce, pine, eucalyptus and holly around the wreath. Leave the pine branches longer than the other materials to create a bushy effect.

7 Mix in larch branches where they fit and let them sprawl out from the wreath shape. Repeat around the whole ring.

8 When you reach the end, lift the pine branches to tuck the stems under the first bunch.

9 Turn the wreath over and cut the wire with wire cutters. Secure by 'sewing' a couple of stitches into the wrapped wire.

MATERIALS
Metal ring
Floral tape
Myrtle wire, green
Secateurs
Wire cutters

FLOWERS/FOLIAGE
Eucalyptus with berries
Holly
Larch
Pine
Spruce

Asymmetric wreath with a dash of pink

I love asymmetric wreaths, even if it can be a bit tricky to get the form right. My simple tip is to cover two thirds of the ring; this will create a harmonious impression. I love pine, preferably sparse and a little bit pointy; I use it for both vases and wreaths.

A dash of pink in the form of pink pepper berries gives a nice contrast both in colour and shape.

LEVEL: ADVANCED

1 Start by wrapping two-thirds of the metal ring with floral tape. Pull the tape lightly so that it gets tacky and sticks to the ring.

2 Attach myrtle wire to the ring by wrapping it around and twisting the end to secure.

3 Start with a few longer branches of pine. Add to the ring and secure in place by wrapping them with myrtle wire.

4 Continue with bunches of sawara cypress, eucalyptus and pink pepper berries in the same way. Make sure to place the plants over the stems of previous bunches so that the stems are hidden.

5 Wrap material around the wreath until you come to just before where the floral tape ends.

6 Take some pine branches and place them the other way around, with the stems against the previous bunches.

7 Continue placing a few more bunches in the opposite direction as in the previous step.

8 Finally, place some more material the same way as you started with and wrap it in place so that the last bit of the floral tape is hidden. Tuck the stems under to hide them.

9 Turn the wreath over and cut the wire with wire cutters. Secure by 'sewing' a couple of stitches into the wrapped wire.

MATERIALS
Metal ring
Floral tape
Myrtle wire, green
Wire cutters

FLOWERS/FOLIAGE
Eucalyptus
Pine
Pink pepper berries
Sawara cypress

Amaryllis wreath

For me, amaryllis has got to be the star of Christmas. I prefer amaryllis as cut flowers as opposed to planted in a pot. This magnificent flower will last for a long time in a vase and, in bouquets, I usually pair it with pine. The flowers also go well with eucalyptus.

Their hollow stems mean they're great for hanging upside down; you can give them water by pouring it directly into the stem. Together with some pine branches, it becomes a beautiful wall decoration.

LEVEL: ADVANCED

1 Start by attaching silver myrtle wire to the ring by wrapping it around and twisting the end.

2 Add some bunches of pine to the ring and wrap the wire a couple of times around the ends. Secure them in more places if needed.

3 Continue the same way with more pine branches around the ring, to cover about two-thirds of the ring.

4 Place amaryllis onto the bare section of the ring and secure at the top with string.

5 Repeat with another three amaryllis flowers. It can look nice to position them at different heights to keep the wreath visually interesting.

6 Cut the stems so that they are on the same level.

7 Don't forget to water the flowers regularly directly into the stems.

MATERIALS
Metal ring
Myrtle wire, silver
String

FLOWERS/FOLIAGE
Amaryllis
Pine

Classic wreath in silver tones

An Advent wreath made on a straw base is what I always recommend as a starting project for those who haven't made wreaths before. The straw base makes it possible to pull the wire properly when making the wreath. Spruce is an easy material to work with and also fills out the wreath well.

In my version of a classic wreath, I add silvery details such as tangly cushion bush and beautiful eucalyptus leaves.

LEVEL: MEDIUM

1 Attach the reel wire to the straw base by wrapping it around the base and twisting the end.

2 Use secateurs to cut spruce into suitable-sized pieces; if you turn the spruce over and cut from the back, it will make the cut surface less visible. It's also easier to see the different parts of the spruce from the back.

3 Start adding spruce to the outside of the wreath, securing in place by wrapping the reel wire around it. Use longer spruce branches on the outside of the wreath and shorter towards the middle.

4 Continue with spruce on the top of the wreath and on the inside the same way. The straw base should be covered completely with spruce, while the back of the base should be left bare.

5 Place bunches of eucalyptus on top of the spruce and secure in place with the reel wire.

6 Continue placing eucalyptus and cushion bush the same way around the whole wreath, dotting some eucalyptus with berries here and there. Place the plants over the stems of the previous bunches to hide them.

7 Turn the wreath over and cut the wire with wire cutters. Secure by 'sewing' a couple of stitches into the wrapped wire.

MATERIALS
Straw base
Reel wire
Secateurs
Wire cutters

FLOWERS/FOLIAGE
Cushion bush
Eucalyptus
Eucalyptus with
  berries
Spruce

Moss table wreath

Wreaths don't always have to be hung up; I often place them on tables, both inside and outside.

I love moss and like to bring it into my home, even if it can get a bit messy. If it starts to dry out, I spray it gently with water. The branches in this wreath are easy to swap out if they start to look tired. Echeveria prefers an indoor climate; if it's below zero it will freeze and will become spongy.

LEVEL: EASY

1 Start by attaching the myrtle wire to the straw base by wrapping it around and twisting the end.

2 Add moss to the wreath to cover the base. Secure it in place with myrtle wire, but don't pull too tightly or the wire will be visible.

3 Add more moss and continue the same way until the whole wreath is completely covered.

4 Turn the wreath over and cut the wire. Secure it in place by 'sewing' a couple of stitches into the wrapped wire.

5 Remove soil and roots from the echeveria by holding the flower in one hand and the soil in the other and twisting.

6 Insert florist wire through the lower part of the plant and bend it into two 'legs'.

7 Attach the echeveria to the wreath by pushing the florist wire into the base. It looks nice when you group several together in a cluster.

8 Cut smaller lengths of florist wire and bend them into u-shapes.

9 Attach branches of eucalyptus and sawara cypress to the wreath using the u-shapes of florist wire.

10 Place the wreath on the table, either directly or on a plate. Place candle holders in the middle of the wreath for an impressive centrepiece.

MATERIALS
Straw base
Myrtle wire, green
Florist wire
Wire cutters

FLOWERS/FOLIAGE
Echeveria
Eucalyptus
Moss
Sawara cypress

Wreath with red berries

In my garden there is a beautiful crab apple tree. At the beginning of the summer, it enriches the garden with lovely flowers, and in the autumn with the cutest little apples. I like to use both of these for wreaths and other decorations. Together with moss, they get to play the main part in this horizontal wreath.

LEVEL: EASY

1 Start by attaching the green myrtle wire to the straw base by wrapping it around the wreath and twisting the end.

2 Add moss to the wreath to cover the base. Secure it in place by carefully wrapping the wire around it, making sure you don't pull too tightly or the wire will be visible.

3 Repeat around the whole wreath to fully cover it in moss.

4 Turn the wreath over and cut the wire. Secure by 'sewing' a couple of stitches into the wrapped wire.

5 Attach silver-coloured myrtle wire in the same way as in step 1.

6 Using secateurs, cut a cushion bush plant into smaller pieces.

7 Place cushion bush on top of the wreath, then secure in place by wrapping it with silver-coloured myrtle wire.

8 Repeat around the whole wreath.

9 Turn the wreath over and cut the wire. Secure by 'sewing' a couple of stitches into the wrapped wire.

10 Insert a length of florist wire through the bottom part of each crab apple and bend it into two 'legs'.

11 Remove the leaves from the St John's wort berries.

12 Attach crab apples closely together on top of the wreath by pushing the florist wires into the base. Continue around the whole wreath.

13 Place St John's wort berries between the crab apples and secure in place with u-shaped florist wire.

MATERIALS
Straw base
Myrtle wire, green
Wire cutters
Myrtle wire, silver
Secateurs
Florist wire

FLOWERS/FOLIAGE
Crab apple
Cushion bush
Moss
St John's wort berries

Cone candle wreath

I like to set the table nicely with a beautiful wreath as a centrepiece. Pine branches keep very well indoors, even if they will of course dry out more quickly due to the warmth. This is a wreath I save and bring out again year after year. A wreath made from cones will keep forever; I just swap out the pine branches each year and the wreath is like new again.

LEVEL: EASY

1 Start by gluing spruce cones to the outside of the straw base using a glue gun.

2 Place cones around the whole wreath so that the outside is completely covered.

3 Add pine branches to the inside of the wreath and secure in place with florist wire.

4 Make sure that the whole of the inside is covered, so that you can't see the straw base coming through.

5 Place pine branches on the top of the wreath. Secure the branches into place using u-shaped lengths of florist wire.

6 Attach florist wire to the pine cones, then push them into the top of the wreath.

7 Push candle holders down into the wreath, then place candles in the candle holders to create a beautiful centrepiece for your table.

MATERIALS
Glue gun
Straw base
Florist wire
Wire cutters
Candle holders

FLOWERS/FOLIAGE
Pine branches
Pine cones with florist wire attached
Spruce cones

Icy winter wreath

When the cold January wind is whistling and the Christmas wreaths have been tidied away, it's nice to cheer yourself up with something light and crisp, such as a wreath in icy tones. In this wreath, I have mixed white and silver with a dash of blue and purple. A few picked plants, such as dried grass and silver dust from the garden, are mixed with some bought flowers, for example blue sea holly. I let the Spanish moss hang down a little, to create a natural feel, and I leave the dried bougainvillea sticking out in this asymmetrical wreath.

LEVEL: ADVANCED

1 Start by wrapping a metal ring with floral tape. Secure the tape and pull it lightly so that it gets tacky and sticks to the ring. Wrap around the whole ring to prevent the flowers from sliding around.

2 Attach myrtle wire to the ring by wrapping it around the ring and then twisting it.

3 Start with the silver dust: it is soft and a bit bushy, which makes it easier to build the rest of the wreath on top of it.

4 Secure the silver dust in place by wrapping the myrtle wire a couple of times around the stems.

5 Continue placing the other materials around the wreath, wrapping them with myrtle wire. Make sure the stems of the previous bunches are covered when you place the next bunch.

6 Repeat around the whole wreath, alternating the materials as you go. For the wreath in the picture, I have grouped different plants together in different parts of the wreath, to give some visual variety. To make the wreath bushy, try to use materials of mixed lengths.

7 When you reach the end, lift the first layer of silver dust and tuck the stems under to hide them.

8 Turn the wreath over and cut the wire with wire cutters. Secure by 'sewing' a couple of stitches into the wrapped wire.

MATERIALS
Metal ring
Floral tape
Myrtle wire, green
Wire cutters

FLOWERS/FOLIAGE
Bougainvillea, dried
Dried butcher's broom
Hare's tail grass
Reed or dried grass
Sea holly, blue
Silver dust
Spanish moss
Wavyleaf sea lavender

FLOWERS

Late summer often brings an abundance of beautiful flowers. I like to grow varieties that can be dried and preserve the flowers for autumn and winter wreaths. Many of these also retain their colour well when dried.

I pick the flowers when they are dry – as in not wet from rain or dew – often in the evening after a fine day.

It's also important to pick the flowers at the right stage; I try to pick them just as they have come out in bloom. Flowers that have been left for even a few days too long will drop their petals more easily.

Many seed pods, such as scabious, are also beautiful and will dry well.

Before I hang up flowers to dry, I pick off most of the leaves, since these rarely look nice once they've dried.

It's cool in my shed, without any direct sunlight, making it the perfect place for drying flowers. Sunlight will bleach the flowers and make them more fragile.

FRUIT

Fruit slices are beautiful in wreaths but they can also be used as decoration in other contexts: in planted pots, in garlands, on Christmas presents. They also smell lovely when dried.

Slices of apple can be dried at room temperature. I slice them thinly, remove the core and hang them on a rod or string with a bit of a gap in between. They will dry in a couple of days. If I want to speed up the process, I place the slices on a tray with baking paper and put them in the oven at 75°C for approximately 5 hours.

There is no lovelier smell than drying oranges. The smell takes me back to the Christmases of my childhood, filled with warmth and wonderful moments. I slice oranges thinly, place the slices on a rack and set the oven to 50–75°C. I then leave them in the oven until they are completely dry, which usually takes 3–5 hours. You can also dry lemons and limes the same way as oranges.

WREATH MATERIALS

When autumn turns into winter and Advent is knocking on the door, I use more evergreen materials for my wreaths.

Different types of spruce, both bought and picked – European spruce, noble spruce with its grey-green colour and Nordmann fir with its silvery back – make great bases for winter wreaths.

In the garden, I have English yew and thuja, both of which are great for wreath making. Different kinds of cypress plants and sugi are also nice. I like to buy sawara cypress, as it has a slightly bluer hue and is soft and not as prickly to work with.

On Öland, there is plenty of juniper and pine and both are among my favourites. The pine has a wonderfully bushy way of growing, which makes it suitable for sprawling wreaths. Juniper often has beautiful berries that shift between blue and green. Juniper is nice, both as the main component in a wreath, or alongside other materials. Remember that you're not allowed to cut branches off growing trees and bushes in nature (see page 120 for more information).

This is the best season for eucalyptus. I love these grey-green leaves that come in so many different varieties. My favourites are the ones with berries, as well as nicholii, which has long and narrow leaves. I also like to use the variety with larger berries on a bare stem. Eucalyptus can be expensive, so I often only use it as decoration together with other materials, such as different kinds of spruce.

Other beautiful leaves include grevillea, which has a silvery back and a long, thin, pointy shape. Some varieties of rhododendron have leaves with brown backs, which look nice in a wreath. Varieties with leaves in white-green tones are also beautiful.

Ivy is a recurrent plant in my wreaths all year round. During the winter, I also like to use its black berries. Other berries that can be bought include St John's wort berries, which comes in a wide variety of colours.

Sea holly is a type of thistle that grows in blue and white. It provides the perfect contrast for winter wreaths. Broad-leaved statice is bushy and gives a wreath a playful feel. The plant comes in many different colours, all of which dry beautifully.

I like to use cushion bush, which gives a wintry and icy feel to wreaths. Skimmia berries are another favourite. They come both in red and white, as well as with variegated leaves (meaning leaves that have more than one colour). The small berries and shiny leaves make a nice contrast to conifer plants.

In the winter, I like to decorate with pine and spruce cones, as well as dried slices of orange and apple. It's nice to add some seasonal variety to the wreaths.

Branches and twigs are personal favourites of mine. I like to use branches of larch, sloe or spruce that are covered in moss.

217

WINTER REST

Eucalyptus boule

Pink pepper berries

Japanese cedar

Pine

Holly

Cypress

Leucadendron

Sawara
cypress

Viburnum

Noble fir

Spruce

Broad-leaved
statice

Eucalyptus

Skimmia

English yew

Wreath materials throughout the year

**LONGING
FOR SPRING**
Apple branches
Baby's breath
Bilberry stems
Birch branches
Broad-leaved statice*
Cladonia lichen
Common box
Common ivy
Corkscrew hazel
Eucalyptus
Grape hyacinth
Green moss
Hazel
Mimosa
Narcissus
Pussy willow
Reed
Rice flower
Sea holly
Spanish moss
St John's wort
Strawflower
Tulip
Wavyleaf sea lavender*
Willow

**BUDDING
GREENERY**
Baby's breath
Broad-leaved statice
Butcher's broom
Carnation
Chrysanthemum
Clove pink
Common box
Common ivy
Cornflower
Grass
Great masterwort
Lady's mantle
Meadow buttercup

Pistacia
Sea holly
St John's wort
Wavyleaf sea lavender

SUMMER LIGHT
Baby's breath
Billy button
Blue globe-thistle
Broad-leaved statice
Butcher's broom
Common box
Common ivy
Flax
Lamb's ear
Lavender
Oat
Pistacia
Rosemary
Rye
Sage
Sea holly
Spiky fescue
St John's wort
Tansy
Thyme
Wavyleaf sea lavender
Wheat

HARVEST TIME
Blackberries
Broad-leaved statice
Brunia
Cladonia lichen
Common ivy
Common snowberry
Cushion bush
Dipsacaceae
Elderberry
Eucalyptus
Fern
Green moss

Heather
Hydrangea
Leucadendron
Maple
Oak
Orpine
Reed
Rosehips
Rowan berries
Sea holly
Spanish moss
St John's wort
Strawflower
Swedish whitebeam
  berries
Wavyleaf sea lavender

WINTER REST
Apple slices
Broad-leaved statice
Brunia
Cladonia lichen
Common box
Common ivy
Common snowberry
Crab apple
Cushion bush
Cypress
Dipsacaceae
English yew
Eucalyptus
Eucalyptus boule
Green moss
Grevillea
Holly
Japanese cedar
Juniper
Larch branches
Larch cone
Leucadendron
Lingonberry stems
Noble fir
Nordmann fir

Orange slices
Pine
Pine cone
Rhododendron
Rosehips
Sawara cypress
Sea holly
Sloe branches
Spanish moss
Spruce
Spruce cone
St John's wort

* *Broad-leaved statice
  and wavyleaf sea
  lavender belong to
  the same genus but
  are two different
  flowers, with
  larger and smaller
  flowers. Limonium
  platyphyllum and
  Limonium sinuatum
  respectively.*

Thank you!

This book would not have existed without certain people in my life.
To have someone to bounce ideas back and forth with, and to support me,
has been invaluable.

Sometimes fantastic meetings happen that result in possibilities that
you would never have dreamed of. Without Jenny, Chrille and Ingvar at
Ingvar Strandh's floristry school, I would never have been where I am today.
I am forever grateful to you for the possibilities you have given to me.

My friend Maja, you are always there with beautiful flowers, support and thoughts.
Thank you for coming with advice and feedback and for cheering me on
when I'm in doubt.

Helena, who proofread my drafts for the book and contributed useful advice.
Thank you for putting up with listening to all aspects of this project.

Mum, Inga-Lill, who always helps out, picking up children and
keeping everything running when there isn't enough time.

Above all, my biggest thanks to my family and my children, who have coped with
periods of their mum working many hours and not always being present.

Peter, my partner, my best friend, who always supports all my ideas and puts up with
all the crazy projects I come up with. You cheer me on when things go well and you
catch me when it's difficult. Without your support, nothing is possible.

First published in the United Kingdom
in 2024 by
Batsford
43 Great Ormond Street
London
WC1N 3HZ

An imprint of B.T. Batsford Holdings Limited

Kransar
Text & Photographs © Malin Björkholm
First published by Norstedts, Sweden, in 2023
Published by agreement with Norstedts Agency and Bennet Agency

English edition copyright © B.T. Batsford Ltd, 2024
Translated by Frida Green

ISBN 978 1 849 94920 0

A CIP catalogue record for this book is available from the British Library.

10 9 8 7 6 5 4 3 2 1

Reproduction by Rival Colour Ltd UK
Printed and bound by Toppan Leefung Printing Ltd., China

This book can be ordered direct from the publisher at
www.batsfordbooks.com, or try your local bookshop.